Cambridge
Key English Test
4

WITH ANSWERS

West

Examination pap
University of Can
ESOL Examinations:
English for Speakers of
Other Languages

CAMBRIDGE
UNIVERSITY PRESS

CAMBRIDGE
UNIVERSITY PRESS

University Printing House, Cambridge CB2 8BS, United Kingdom

Cambridge University Press is part of the University of Cambridge.

It furthers the University's mission by disseminating knowledge in the pursuit of education, learning and research at the highest international levels of excellence.

www.cambridge.org
Information on this title: www.cambridge.org/9780521670821

First published 2006
15th printing 2013

A catalogue record for this publication is available from the British Library

ISBN 978-0-521-67082-1 Student's Book with answers
ISBN 978-0-521-67081-4 Student's Book
ISBN 978-0-521-67085-2 Audio Cassette
ISBN 978-0-521-67084-5 Audio CD
ISBN 978-0-521-67083-8 Self-study Pack (Student's Book with answers and Audio CD)

Contents

Acknowledgements

The publishers are grateful for permission to reproduce copyright material. It has not always been possible to identify the sources of all the material used, and in such cases the publishers would welcome information from the copyright owners.

Illustrations by Servis Filmsetting Ltd, Manchester

Book design by Peter Ducker MSTD

Cover design by Dunne & Scully

The cassette/CD which accompanies this book was recorded at Studio AVP, London.

Introduction

This collection of four complete practice tests comprises past papers from the University of Cambridge ESOL Examinations Key English Test (KET) examination; students can practise these tests on their own or with the help of a teacher.

The KET examination is part of a group of examinations developed by Cambridge ESOL called the Cambridge Main Suite. The Main Suite consists of five examinations that have similar characteristics but are designed for different levels of English language ability. Within the five levels, KET is at Level A2 in the *Council of Europe's Common European Framework of Reference for Languages: Learning, teaching, assessment.* It has also been accredited by the Qualifications and Curriculum Authority in the UK as an Entry 2 ESOL certificate in the National Qualifications Framework. The KET examination offers a basic qualification in English and also represents a first step for those wishing to progress towards the Preliminary English Test (PET) and other Cambridge ESOL examinations.

Examination	Council of Europe Framework Level	UK National Qualifications Framework Level
CPE Certificate of Proficiency in English	C2	3
CAE Certificate in Advanced English	C1	2
FCE First Certificate in English	B2	1
PET Preliminary English Test	B1	Entry 3
KET Key English Test	A2	Entry 2

Further information

The information contained in this practice book is designed to be an overview of the exam. For a full description of all the above exams, including information about task types, testing focus and preparation, please see the relevant handbooks which can be obtained from Cambridge ESOL at the address below or from the website at www.cambridgeESOL.org

University of Cambridge ESOL Examinations
1 Hills Road
Cambridge CB1 2EU
United Kingdom
Telephone: +44 1223 553355
Fax: +44 1223 460278
Email: ESOLHelpdesk@ucles.org.uk

The structure of KET: an overview

The KET examination has three papers: Reading and Writing, Listening and Speaking.

Paper 1 Reading and Writing (1 hour 10 minutes)

The Reading and Writing paper has nine parts and a total of 50 marks.

This paper assesses candidates' ability to read and understand factual texts from signs, brochures, newspapers and magazines. For reading, candidates need to be able to understand the main messages, and have ways of dealing with unfamiliar words and structures. For writing, candidates are assessed on their ability to complete gaps in simple texts, transfer information to forms, and complete an everyday writing task, such as a short note or message of around 20–25 words, to show they can use structure, vocabulary, spelling and punctuation.

Paper 2 Listening (approximately 30 minutes including 8 minutes to transfer answers)

The Listening paper has five parts and a total of 25 marks.

This paper assesses candidates' ability to understand recorded material such as announcements and monologues, delivered at a moderate pace, and to understand factual information in the recordings.

Paper 3 Speaking (8–10 minutes)

The Speaking test has two parts and a total of 25 marks.

The test assesses candidates' ability to interact in conversational English with an examiner and with another candidate. Candidates need to be able to answer questions about themselves and to talk freely about their likes and dislikes. Candidates normally take the Speaking test in pairs.

Grading

The Reading and Writing paper carries 50% of the total marks, while the Listening and Speaking tests carry 25% each. There are two pass grades ('Pass with Merit' and 'Pass') and certificates are normally issued to candidates who achieve these grades. A 'Pass' grade usually corresponds to approximately 70% of the total marks, and 'Pass with Merit' to approximately 85%. There is no minimum pass mark for individual papers. Candidates who achieve a 'Narrow Fail' or 'Fail' are judged not to have reached the required standard for KET.

For further information on grading and results, please go to the website (see page 6).

Test 1

PAPER 1 READING AND WRITING (1 hour 10 minutes)

PART 1

QUESTIONS 1–5

Which notice (A–H) says this (1–5)?

For questions 1–5, mark the correct letter A–H on your answer sheet.

Example:

0 You can take your old shirts or trousers here.

Answer:

0	A	B	C	D	E	F	G	H
	☐	☐	☐	☐	☐	☐	☐	■

---

1 These cost less than usual.

A

> KEEP THIS MEDICINE
> AWAY FROM CHILDREN

B

> Check your holiday insurance now –
> *before* you go away.

2 This is a bad time to be ill.

C

> **SORRY!**
> No showers in the Sports Centre this week

3 Be careful where you put this.

D

> **Dr Jenkins is on holiday until Friday.**

4 You will need to take a heavy sweater or jacket with you.

E

> **TODAY**
> Day trip to the mountains
> Wear something warm!

F

> **CAR WASH – £4**
> *We'll make it look like new*

5 You will not be able to wash yourself here for a few days.

G

> All our winter holidays –
> **25% cheaper**

H

> *We buy and sell second-hand clothes.*

PART 2

QUESTIONS 6–10

Read the sentences about cooking a meal.
Choose the best word (A, B or C) for each space.
For questions 6–10, mark A, B or C on your answer sheet.

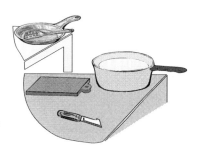

Example:

0 Last week, Louise .... some friends at her new school.

   A   made   **B**   started   **C**   played

Answer:

0	A	B	C
	■	☐	☐

---

6 She .... all of them to dinner at her house on Saturday evening.

   A   phoned   **B**   invited   **C**   said

7 Louise wrote the things she needed to buy for the meal on a .... of paper.

   A   piece   **B**   slice   **C**   part

8 She was .... on Saturday morning so she went shopping in the afternoon.

   A   full   **B**   busy   **C**   difficult

9 Louise .... two hours cooking the meal.

   A   waited   **B**   spent   **C**   passed

10 When the meal was .... , everyone sat down to eat.

   A   right   **B**   sure   **C**   ready

PART 3

QUESTIONS 11–15

Complete the five conversations.

For questions 11–15, mark A, B or C on your answer sheet.

Example:

0

Where do you come from?

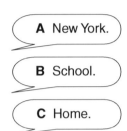

A New York.

B School.

C Home.

Answer:

0	A B C
	■☐☐

---

11 Are you sure the match starts at two?

    A It started well.

    B It's all right.

    C I think so.

12 I saw the new Spielberg film last night.

    A Did I go?

    B Has he come?

    C Was it good?

13 How did the accident happen?

    A I can't go there.

    B I didn't see it.

    C I don't know how to.

14 Hello, I'd like to speak to Mr Green, please.

    A Sorry, can you say that again?

    B I'm sorry, I'll call again later.

    C I'm afraid I don't know.

15 May I leave now?

    A When we've finished.

    B Until tomorrow.

    C I don't agree.

QUESTIONS 16–20

Complete the conversation.
What does Tom say to the receptionist?
For questions 16–20, mark the correct letter A–H on your answer sheet.

Example:

Receptionist: Good evening, can I help you?

Tom: **0** ....

Answer: | **0** | A | B | C | D | E | F | G | H |
|---|---|---|---|---|---|---|---|---|
| | ☐ | ☐ | ■ | ☐ | ☐ | ☐ | ☐ | ☐ |

Receptionist: I'm afraid all our single rooms are full. How long do you want to stay?

Tom: **16** ....

Receptionist: I have a double room for £60.

Tom: **17** ....

Receptionist: I'm sure they're full too. There are a lot of tourists in town at the moment.

Tom: **18** ....

Receptionist: I'm afraid the restaurant is closed. Breakfast starts at 7 tomorrow.

Tom: **19** ....

Receptionist: Your room must be empty by 12 o'clock. But you can put your luggage in reception.

Tom: **20** ....

Receptionist: Would you write your name in the book, please?

A   I see. Can I get something to eat in this hotel?

B   Would you show me the room?

C   I'm looking for a single room.

D   What time does it finish?

E   If I stay here, can I leave my suitcase in my room tomorrow afternoon?

F   That's rather expensive. Are there any other hotels near here?

G   Just for one night.

H   OK. I'll take the room.

PART 4

QUESTIONS 21–27

Read the article about Bill Bryson, a writer.

Are sentences 21–27 'Right' (A) or 'Wrong' (B)?

If there is not enough information to answer 'Right' (A) or 'Wrong' (B), choose 'Doesn't say' (C).

For questions 21–27, mark A, B or C on your answer sheet.

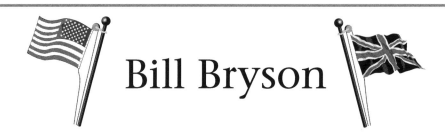

Bill Bryson

I was born in the United States but I have written several travel books about England. I lived there with my wife and four children for 20 years, but for the last three years we have lived in the United States. Our children are now learning about life in the United States. I'm sure they will be happier because they have lived in two countries. I like Britain and I want to return, but my daughter, Felicity, is going to start college here soon, so it won't be for another four years.

I have just been to England for six weeks to work on a radio programme about the English language and also to talk about the book I've just written. Most writers don't like doing this; they don't like travelling around the country, selling their book. I don't mind it. I like visiting new places and meeting lots of people. It's very different from the life I have in the United States when I'm writing. In England, people drove me around in big cars and I stayed in expensive hotels. It was good because I didn't have to pay any bills. Everyone was kind to me and it was fun.

Example:

0   Bill has written about a country he has visited.

    A   Right   **B**   Wrong   **C**   Doesn't say   *Answer:*

---

21   Bill returned to the United States after living in England for a long time.

    A   Right   **B**   Wrong   **C**   Doesn't say

22   Bill thinks it will be good for his children to live in more than one country.

    A   Right   **B**   Wrong   **C**   Doesn't say

23   Bill's daughter didn't want to go to college in England.

    A   Right   **B**   Wrong   **C**   Doesn't say

24   Bill has just visited England to finish writing his new book.

    A   Right   **B**   Wrong   **C**   Doesn't say

25   Bill is happy with the things he has to do to sell his books.

    A   Right   **B**   Wrong   **C**   Doesn't say

26   Bill has travelled to many different places in the United States.

    A   Right   **B**   Wrong   **C**   Doesn't say

27   It cost Bill a lot of money to travel around England for six weeks.

    A   Right   **B**   Wrong   **C**   Doesn't say

PART 5

QUESTIONS 28–35

Read the article about crocodiles.

Choose the best word (A, B or C) for each space.

For questions 28–35, mark A, B or C on your answer sheet.

CROCODILES

We can find crocodiles in tropical parts of **(0)** .... world, for example Africa, South America and Northern Australia.

They spend most of the time **(28)** .... slow-moving water but they **(29)** .... move fast through the water and on land.

You often see crocodiles together in large groups. They **(30)** .... everything they catch, **(31)** .... fish, birds and small animals. And sometimes they make a meal of large animals or even people.

There are **(32)** .... than ten types of crocodile. They all have very sharp teeth. They often lose **(33)** .... teeth, but soon get new ones.

Crocodiles are usually about 3.5 metres long, but some are much **(34)** .... Crocodiles live **(35)** .... a long time. The oldest one kept in a zoo was 66 years old.

Example:

0	**A**	the	**B**	an	**C**	a	*Answer:*

28	**A**	in	**B**	on	**C**	at

29	**A**	are	**B**	can	**C**	have

30	**A**	eats	**B**	eat	**C**	ate

31	**A**	by	**B**	like	**C**	to

32	**A**	more	**B**	most	**C**	many

33	**A**	this	**B**	that	**C**	these

34	**A**	bigger	**B**	big	**C**	biggest

35	**A**	for	**B**	since	**C**	during

PART 6

QUESTIONS 36–40

Read the descriptions of some things you can read.

What is the word for each one?

The first letter is already there. There is one space for each other letter in the word.

For questions 36–40, write the words on your answer sheet.

Example:

0 When your friends go on holiday, they send you this.   **p** __ __ __ __ __ __ __

Answer: | **0** | *p o s t c a r d*

---

36 If you don't understand a word, you can look in this.   **d** __ __ __ __ __ __ __ __ __

37 You can buy this every week and read about many interesting subjects in it.   **m** __ __ __ __ __ __ __

38 If you write about your daily life in this, you may not want anyone to read it.   **d** __ __ __ __

39 You write this for your mother when you answer the phone for her.   **m** __ __ __ __ __ __

40 People buy this every morning to read about what has happened in the world.   **n** __ __ __ __ __ __ __ __

PART 7

QUESTIONS 41–50

Complete the letter.
Write ONE word for each space.
For questions 41–50, write the words on your answer sheet.

Example: | **0** | *be* |

Paris

Dear Maria,

It's good to **(0)** .... back home in my country but I still think **(41)** ....
all the friends I made in our English class, especially you. I cried **(42)** ....
I left England because my visit **(43)** .... too short. I would **(44)** .... to
return to England but **(45)** .... time I will stay in a different city.

I have started English classes again here. I learnt a **(46)** .... of things in
England but I know I **(47)** .... to study even harder.

(48) .... about you? **(49)** .... you still looking for a job? I hope you find
(50) .... soon.

Love,

Sophie

PART 8

QUESTIONS 51–55

Read the letter from Jane Harvey.

Fill in the information on the Lost Property Report Form.

For questions 51–55, write the information on your answer sheet.

The Manager   16 March
North Line Trains
London

Dear Sir,

On 14 March, I got on the 12.45 train to London at Manchester station. I had a suitcase and a handbag with me. When I got off the train at 14.50, I did not have my handbag.

Has anyone found it? Please phone me on 723419 or, after 6 p.m., on 796327.

Jane Harvey

LOST PROPERTY REPORT FORM

Name of passenger:	Jane Harvey
Travelling from:	**51**
Date of journey:	**52**
Time journey started:	**53**
What did you lose?	**54**
Daytime phone number:	**55**

PART 9

QUESTION 56

Read this note from your friend, Spencer.

> Let's meet for dinner near your house on Saturday.
>
> Where shall we eat? What time can you come? Where can I park my car?
>
> Spencer

Write Spencer a note. Answer the questions.

Write 25–35 words.

Write the note on your answer sheet.

PAPER 2 LISTENING (approximately 30 minutes including 8 minutes transfer time)

PART 1

QUESTIONS 1–5

You will hear five short conversations.

You will hear each conversation twice.

There is one question for each conversation.

For questions 1–5, put a tick (✔) under the right answer.

Example:

0 How many people were at the meeting?

3	**13**	**30**
A ☐	B ☐	C ✔

---

1 What music will they have at the party?

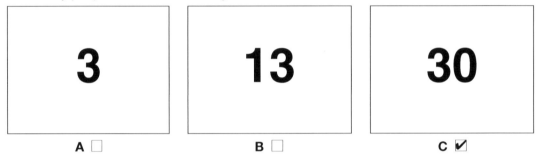

| A ☐ | B ☐ | C ☐ |

2 When will the man go on holiday?

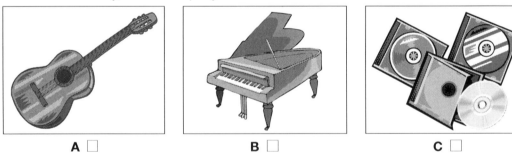

June	**July**	**August**
A ☐	B ☐	C ☐

3   What will the weather be like tomorrow?

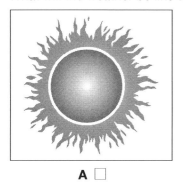      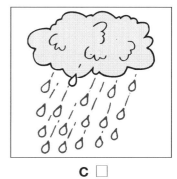

A ☐   **B** ☐   **C** ☐

4   What colour is Mary's coat?

A ☐   **B** ☐   **C** ☐

5   What did the woman repair?

A ☐   **B** ☐   **C** ☐

PART 2

QUESTIONS 6–10

Listen to Sarah talking to a friend about her holiday photographs.
What place is each person in?
For questions 6–10, write a letter A–H next to each person.
You will hear the conversation twice.

Example:

0   Sarah's mother   E

People

6   Caroline

7   Jack

8   Sarah

9   Peter

10 Sarah's father

Places

A   castle

B   cathedral

C   hotel

D   market

E   mountains

F   museum

G   restaurant

H   sea

PART 3

QUESTIONS 11–15

Listen to Sue talking to her friend, Jim, about the new sports centre.
For questions 11–15, tick (✔) A, B or C.
You will hear the conversation twice.

Example:

0	The new sports centre is	A	cheap.	☐
		B	big.	✔
		C	dark.	☐

11	Which bus goes to the sports centre?	A	15	☐
		B	18	☐
		C	25	☐

12	From Monday to Saturday, the sports centre is open from	A	6 a.m.	☐
		B	7 a.m.	☐
		C	9 a.m.	☐

13	If Sue goes swimming, she must take	A	soap.	☐
		B	a swimming hat.	☐
		C	a towel.	☐

14 At the sports centre, you can buy

    A sandwiches. ☐

    B fruit. ☐

    C drinks. ☐

15 Jim and Sue are going to go to the sports centre next

    A Wednesday. ☐

    B Thursday. ☐

    C Saturday. ☐

PART 4

QUESTIONS 16–20

You will hear a man making a telephone call.

Listen and complete questions 16–20.

You will hear the conversation twice.

MESSAGE

To:	Diana
From:	Ian
Name of hotel:	**16**
Address:	**17** .... *Street*
Meeting starts at:	**18**
Bring:	**19**
Visit factory on:	**20**

PART 5

QUESTIONS 21–25

You will hear some information about a zoo.
Listen and complete questions 21–25.
You will hear the information twice.

Park Zoo

Monday–Saturday, open from:	*9 a.m.*
to:	**21**
Name of nearest station:	**22** .... *Station*
Elephant House closed on:	**23** .... *May*
Shop sells books, postcards and:	**24**
Cost of family ticket:	**25** *£*

You now have 8 minutes to write your answers on the answer sheet.

PAPER 3 SPEAKING (8–10 minutes)

The Speaking test lasts 8 to 10 minutes. You will take the test with another candidate. There are two examiners, but only one of them will talk to you. The examiner will ask you questions and ask you to talk to the other candidate.

Part 1 (5–6 minutes)

The examiner will ask you and your partner some questions. These questions will be about your daily life, past experience and future plans. For example, you may have to speak about your school, job, hobbies or home town.

Part 2 (3–4 minutes)

You and your partner will speak to each other. You will ask and answer questions. The examiner will give you a card with some information on it. The examiner will give your partner a card with some words on it. Your partner will use the words on the card to ask you questions about the information you have. Then you will change roles.

Test 2

PAPER 1   READING AND WRITING (1 hour 10 minutes)

PART 1

QUESTIONS 1–5

Which notice (A–H) says this (1–5)?

For questions 1–5, mark the correct letter A–H on your answer sheet.

Example:

0   Adults cannot sit here.

Answer:

---

1   If you have a second class ticket, you can't go in here.

A   SEATS AT THE FRONT RESERVED FOR CHILDREN

B   SATURDAY – SUNDAY
Travel First Class
at Second Class prices

2   You should wait here before you sit down.

C   **Waiting Room closed for cleaning**

D   —— TRAINS ——
For a seat, book early
(one week in advance)

3   There are no more seats for the show.

E   WAITING ROOM
For passengers with First Class tickets

4   If you want a seat, get your ticket seven days before you travel.

F   QUEEN'S THEATRE
ALL TICKETS SOLD OUT
STANDING ROOM ONLY

G   Please wait for a waitress to show you to your seat.

5   First class tickets are cheaper at the weekend.

H   *THIS WEEK ONLY!*
Buy two full-price tickets –
get one half-price!

PART 2

QUESTIONS 6–10

Read the sentences about cooking.
Choose the best word (A, B or C) for each space.
For questions 6–10, mark A, B or C on your answer sheet.

Example:

0 I like to .... my mother in the kitchen.

    A work   **B** help   **C** stay

Answer:

0	A	B	C
	☐	■	☐

---

6 My mother often asks me to .... up the vegetables for her.

    A put   **B** make   **C** cut

7 Everybody in our family .... fish to meat.

    A enjoys   **B** likes   **C** prefers

8 Once, I forgot the cooker was hot and .... my hand.

    A boiled   **B** burnt   **C** fried

9 Cooking a good meal can .... a long time.

    A spend   **B** use   **C** take

10 At the supermarket, some food like pizza is .... to cook.

    A right   **B** ready   **C** free

PART 3

QUESTIONS 11–15

Complete the five conversations.

For questions 11–15, mark A, B or C on your answer sheet.

Example:

0

Where do you come from?

A New York.

B School.

C Home.

Answer: 0   A B C ■□□

---

11 Let's listen to this new CD.

A Who's the singer?

B It's in the record shop.

C I can hear it.

12 I'd like two tickets for tonight.

A I'll just check for you.

B Afternoon and evening.

C How much did you pay?

13 What time did the meeting end?

A In a minute.

B For half an hour.

C Just before lunch.

14 I can't do this maths problem.

A I suppose so.

B Let me see.

C Certainly not.

15 Do you like Jane's new flat?

A I don't go there.

B She likes the new house.

C The rooms are rather small.

QUESTIONS 16–20

Complete the conversation between two friends outside a cinema.
What does Mary say to Sarah?
For questions 16–20, mark the correct letter A–H on your answer sheet.

Example:

Sarah: Hi, Mary. Sorry I'm late.

Mary: **0** ....

Answer:

	0	A	B	C	D	E	F	G	H
		☐	☐	☐	☐	■	☐	☐	☐

Sarah: Where's John?

Mary: **16** ....

Sarah: The traffic is very bad.

Mary: **17** ....

Sarah: Oh, that's right. He doesn't like driving at night. Well, let's phone him. Have you got his number?

Mary: **18** ....

Sarah: Oh dear, that's a pity. We won't see the beginning of the film. It starts in five minutes.

Mary: **19** ....

Sarah: I'll see you inside then.

Mary: **20** ....

Sarah: Yes, and I'll get some chocolates too. See you in a minute.

A   No, it's in my diary at work.

B   Can you get me an orange juice?

C   Yes, I have. I'll phone him now.

D   Why don't you go in? I've got John's ticket so I'll wait here.

E   Oh, that's all right.

F   If he doesn't come in five minutes, let's go in.

G   He's late too. I told him to be here at seven.

H   I think he's coming by train.

PART 4

QUESTIONS 21–27

Read the article about the sport of snowboarding.

Are sentences 21–27 'Right' (A) or 'Wrong' (B)?

If there is not enough information to answer 'Right' (A) or 'Wrong' (B), choose 'Doesn't say' (C).

For questions 21–27, mark A, B or C on your answer sheet.

— Snowboarding —

Victoria Jamieson from Britain started snowboarding at 20. She is now 23 and has won many competitions in this sport. We spoke to her when she was at a snowboarding competition last week in Switzerland and asked her why she started the sport.

'I've always liked all kinds of sports, especially skiing, and it seemed natural to start snowboarding. It doesn't take long to learn and you can become really good in a few months.'

We asked her if she had to do a lot of practice. 'Well, in winter I snowboard in the mountains every day from 8.30 a.m. until 4 p.m. I also run and go biking. But I just love doing it all! I like the competitions and being in the mountains. It's so beautiful. But free-riding, that's doing what you want when you're not in a competition, is the best thing in the world for me.'

We asked her what is important when you're learning. 'You can learn quickly but you need lessons. It's also important to have the right clothes so you don't get wet because, to begin with, you spend a lot of time falling down!'

Example:

0   Victoria began snowboarding when she was 23.

   A   Right   **B**   Wrong   **C**   Doesn't say   *Answer:* | **0** | A B C |

---

21   Victoria was visiting Switzerland for a competition.

   A   Right   **B**   Wrong   **C**   Doesn't say

22   Victoria has won many skiing competitions.

   A   Right   **B**   Wrong   **C**   Doesn't say

23   Victoria thinks that snowboarding is a difficult sport to learn.

   A   Right   **B**   Wrong   **C**   Doesn't say

24   Working hard at her sport is not a problem for Victoria.

   A   Right   **B**   Wrong   **C**   Doesn't say

25   Victoria likes competitions more than anything else.

   A   Right   **B**   Wrong   **C**   Doesn't say

26   Victoria thinks you should have a teacher if you want to learn snowboarding.

   A   Right   **B**   Wrong   **C**   Doesn't say

27   Victoria says you can wear anything you like when you learn to snowboard.

   A   Right   **B**   Wrong   **C**   Doesn't say

PART 5

QUESTIONS 28–35

Read the article about bears.
Choose the best word (A, B or C) for each space.
For questions 28–35, mark A, B or C on your answer sheet.

The bear can **(0)** .... a dangerous animal. The adult bear is very strong and it can kill a person. Bears are good at **(28)** .... trees and they can run very fast. But they cannot see well and, **(29)** .... most animals, they find food by using **(30)** .... noses.

There are seven kinds of bear. The **(31)** .... is the white polar bear, which is almost three metres tall. There are two kinds of black bear. **(32)** .... lives in the forests of North America, and the other lives in South-East Asia. But not **(33)** .... black bears are black. They may be dark brown or a reddish brown.

Everyone loves the black and white panda bear, which comes from China. Not **(34)** .... pandas live in the forest today because **(35)** .... is difficult to find food.

Example:

0	**A**	is	**B**	being	**C**	be	*Answer:*	0	A B C

28	**A**	climbed	**B**	climb	**C**	climbing
29	**A**	like	**B**	from	**C**	for
30	**A**	them	**B**	those	**C**	their
31	**A**	larger	**B**	largest	**C**	large
32	**A**	Both	**B**	One	**C**	He
33	**A**	every	**B**	all	**C**	each
34	**A**	many	**B**	more	**C**	much
35	**A**	there	**B**	anything	**C**	it

PART 6

QUESTIONS 36–40

Read the descriptions of some feelings.
What is the word for each one?
The first letter is already there. There is one space for each other letter in the word.
For questions 36–40, write the words on your answer sheet.

Example:

0 If you do not wear a coat outside in the snow, you feel
like this.   c __ __ __

Answer:	**0**	*c o l d*

---

36 People feel like this when they get good news.   h __ __ __ __

37 If you have worked hard all day, you feel like this.   t __ __ __ __

38 When you have finished playing football, you want a   d __ __ __ __
shower because you feel like this.

39 If people go without a meal all day, they begin to feel like   h __ __ __ __ __
this.

40 You feel like this if it is hot and there is nothing to drink.   t __ __ __ __ __ __

PART 7

QUESTIONS 41–50

Complete these letters.
Write ONE word for each space.
For questions 41–50, write the words on your answer sheet.

Example: | **0** | *next* |

Dear David,

I'm going to visit your country **(0)** .... month. I'm going to travel
(41) .... two friends. We don't know **(42)** .... to stay. Are **(43)** ....
any cheap hotels in your town? We **(44)** .... like to stay somewhere in the
centre. Can **(45)** .... help us?

Carlos

Dear Carlos,

Hotels in the centre **(46)** .... expensive, but I have good news. I
(47) .... spoken to my aunt Gloria about you and she says you can all stay
at **(48)** .... house. It **(49)** .... more bedrooms than my house! That
(50) .... be all right for you, won't it?

David

PART 8

QUESTIONS 51–55

Read the note and the ticket.

Fill in the information in Mary's diary.

For questions 51–55, write the information on your answer sheet.

Monday

Mary,

Did you get to your 10 o'clock dentist appointment this morning?

Here's your ticket for Wednesday night (give me the money then).

Jack phoned – Castle Restaurant is closed on Tuesday, so he'll see you at Bridges Café at 12.45.

See you for tennis this afternoon.

Love, Sam

CONCERT TICKET

Spanish Guitar Evening

Wednesday, 23 June   **7.45 p.m.**

£16.50   **SEAT: R 12**

MARY'S DIARY

Monday:	10.00 a.m.		Dentist appointment
	2.30–3.30 p.m.	**51**	.... with Sam
Tuesday:	12.45 p.m.	**52**	Lunch with ....
		53	Meet in ....
Wednesday:	7.45 p.m.	**54**	Concert of .... music
	Give Sam:	**55**	.... for my ticket

PART 9

QUESTION 56

Read this note from your new penfriend, Alex.

Hello. I'm Alex, your new penfriend. How old are you? Have you got any brothers and sisters? What is your favourite hobby?

Alex

Write a note to Alex. Answer the questions.
Write 25–35 words.
Write the note on your answer sheet.

PAPER 2 LISTENING (approximately 30 minutes including 8 minutes transfer time)

PART 1

QUESTIONS 1–5

You will hear five short conversations.

You will hear each conversation twice.

There is one question for each conversation.

For questions 1–5, put a tick (✔) under the right answer.

Example:

0   How many people were at the meeting?

3	**13**	**30**
A ☐	B ☐	C ✔

---

1   What are they going to buy for Pam?

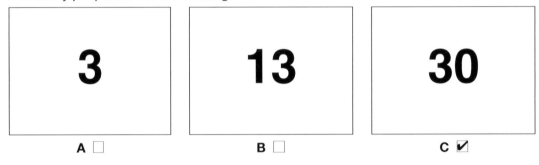

A ☐	B ☐	C ☐

2   When is the man's appointment?

Wednesday	Thursday	Friday
A ☐	B ☐	C ☐

3   Which is the aunt's postcard?

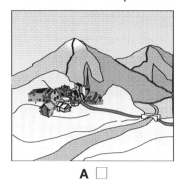      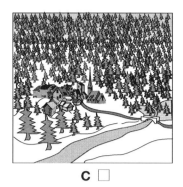

A ☐   B ☐   C ☐

4   What time will the plane to Milan leave?

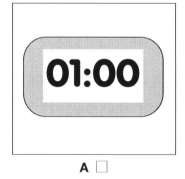      

A ☐   B ☐   C ☐

5   What does Joe's father do?

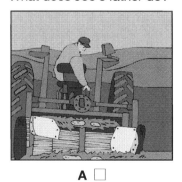      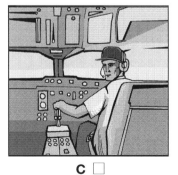

A ☐   B ☐   C ☐

PART 2

QUESTIONS 6–10

Listen to Sarah and Matthew talking about the people they met at a party.
What do they say about each person?
For questions 6–10, write a letter A–H next to each person.
You will hear the conversation twice.

Example:

0 Jenny **A**

People

6 John

7 Mary

8 Bob

9 David

10 Sally

Descriptions

A blonde

B famous

C friendly

D interesting

E quiet

F short

G tall

H young

PART 3

QUESTIONS 11–15

Listen to Anne asking her friend about going to a shopping centre.
For questions 11–15, tick (✔) A, B or C.
You will hear the conversation twice.

Example:

0   The name of the new shopping centre is

A   The Rivers. ☐

B   The Forest Centre. ☐

C   Queen's. ✔

---

11   At the moment, the shopping centre sells

A   clothes. ☐

B   books. ☐

C   food. ☐

12   You can take a coach to the shopping centre on

A   Mondays. ☐

B   Tuesdays. ☐

C   Saturdays. ☐

13   Anne's coach ticket will cost

A   £2.50. ☐

B   £5.60. ☐

C   £10.80. ☐

14   The nearest coach stop to Anne's house is

   A   in the bus station.   ☐

   B   in the market square.   ☐

   C   outside the museum.   ☐

15   The coach journey takes

   A   10 minutes.   ☐

   B   20 minutes.   ☐

   C   40 minutes.   ☐

PART 4

QUESTIONS 16–20

You will hear a telephone conversation about a journey to New York.

Listen and complete questions 16–20.

You will hear the conversation twice.

JOHN LOCKE TRAVEL

Travel to:		New York
Name:	**16**	Mr ....
Will leave on:	**17**	.... December
Will return on:	**18**	30th ....
Price:	**19**	£
Travel to airport by:	**20**	

PART 5

QUESTIONS 21–25

You will hear Susanna leaving a phone message for her mother.

Listen and complete questions 21–25.

You will hear the information twice.

Message

From:	Susanna
Buy:	**21** a white ....
Name of shop:	**22**
In High Street, next to:	**23**
Size:	**24**
Price:	**25** £

You now have 8 minutes to write your answers on the answer sheet.

PAPER 3   SPEAKING (8–10 minutes)

The Speaking test lasts 8 to 10 minutes. You will take the test with another candidate. There are two examiners, but only one of them will talk to you. The examiner will ask you questions and ask you to talk to the other candidate.

Part 1 (5–6 minutes)

The examiner will ask you and your partner some questions. These questions will be about your daily life, past experience and future plans. For example, you may have to speak about your school, job, hobbies or home town.

Part 2 (3–4 minutes)

You and your partner will speak to each other. You will ask and answer questions. The examiner will give you a card with some information on it. The examiner will give your partner a card with some words on it. Your partner will use the words on the card to ask you questions about the information you have. Then you will change roles.

Test 3

PAPER 1   READING AND WRITING (1 hour 10 minutes)

PART 1

QUESTIONS 1–5

Which notice (A–H) says this (1–5)?
For questions 1–5, mark the correct letter A–H on your answer sheet.

Example:

0   You can't pay by cheque.

Answer:

0	A	B	C	D	E	F	G	H
	☐	■	☐	☐	☐	☐	☐	☐

---

1   You can't leave your car here all day.

A   **ROAD CLOSED**
BECAUSE OF TRAFFIC ACCIDENT

B   **SORRY –
CASH ONLY**

2   You pay less to eat at this time.

C   **SHORT STAY CAR PARK**
£1.50 up to 2 hours

3   If you are staying here, you may leave your car in this place.

D   **TWO MEALS FOR THE PRICE
OF ONE WITH THIS VOUCHER**

E   **PARKING FOR HOTEL
GUESTS ONLY**

4   Bring a friend here for lunch and you will pay for only one meal.

F    CROSSROADS CAFÉ
Good, cheap food 24 hours a day

5   You cannot drive here at the moment.

G   **All meals HALF-PRICE
5–6 pm**

H   **LAST PETROL STATION
BEFORE MOTORWAY**

PART 2

QUESTIONS 6–10

Read the sentences about going shopping.
Choose the best word (A, B or C) for each space.
For questions 6–10, mark A, B or C on your answer sheet.

Example:

0 Susan .... to go shopping last Saturday morning.

    A liked   **B** wanted   **C** thought

Answer:	0	A	B	C
		☐	■	☐

---

6 Her friend Carol .... she'd like to go too.

    A said   **B** told   **C** asked

7 At the shopping centre they went up in the .... to the shops on the second floor.

    A street   **B** stairs   **C** lift

8 Susan tried on some shoes but they were the .... colour.

    A bad   **B** wrong   **C** dark

9 They stopped in a café for a drink and a .... of cake.

    A part   **B** little   **C** piece

10 The café was .... but they didn't have to wait a long time.

    A fast   **B** busy   **C** late

PART 3

QUESTIONS 11–15

Complete the five conversations.

For questions 11–15, mark A, B or C on your answer sheet.

Example:

0

How are you?

A I'm 18.

B I'm Sally.

C I'm fine.

Answer: 0   A B C

---

11   How did you go to Madrid?

    A   On Wednesday.

    B   By plane.

    C   It's expensive.

12   I really must go now!

    A   How long is it?

    B   Can't you stay?

    C   What time?

13   Is Mike still doing his homework?

    A   Yes, he does.

    B   It's ready.

    C   Let's ask him.

14   I can't understand this letter.

    A   Would you like some help?

    B   Don't you know?

    C   I suppose you can.

15   Are you sure the film starts at 10?

    A   Yes, I am.

    B   No, I didn't.

    C   Yes, I do.

QUESTIONS 16–20

Complete the conversation.

What does Sally say to the journalist?

For questions 16–20, mark the correct letter A–H on your answer sheet.

Example:

Journalist: I'm from the *Daily News*. Can you tell me what happened
               to you in the storm last night?

Sally: **0** ....

Answer: | **0** | A | B | C | D | E | F | G | H |
            |-------|---|---|---|---|---|---|---|---|
            | | □ | □ | □ | ■ | □ | □ | □ | □ |

Journalist: When did the thunderstorm start?

Sally: **16** ....

Journalist: And when do you usually go to bed?

Sally: **17** ....

Journalist: So before you went to sleep, you
               heard a noise in the garden?

Sally: **18** ....

Journalist: Were you afraid?

Sally: **19** ....

Journalist: And how old was the tree?

Sally: **20** ....

Journalist: Well, it's an interesting story. Thanks
               for talking to me.

A   That's right, I did. I ran out and
       saw a tree fall on the house.

B   When I was tired, yes.

C   At eleven most nights.

D   If you like. What do you want to
       know?

E   That's the sad thing. It's been in
       the garden for about two
       hundred years and many birds
       lived in it.

F   I'm not sure, but it was after I
       went to bed.

G   I don't know. About ten minutes.

H   I was at first, until I saw nobody
       was hurt.

PART 4

QUESTIONS 21–27

Read the article about ice-fishing.

Are sentences 21–27 'Right' (A) or 'Wrong' (B)?

If there is not enough information to answer 'Right' (A) or 'Wrong' (B), choose 'Doesn't say' (C).

For questions 21–27, mark A, B or C on your answer sheet.

If you drive north from Toronto for three hours, you come to Lake Nipissing. In winter, the lake becomes ice, and thousands of Canadian fishermen travel there each weekend. They build little houses of wood on the ice and paint them in bright colours. Then they sit inside to catch the fish that swim under the ice.

Bob Marvisch has come here at this time of year for twenty-five years. 'You need clothes that are light but warm: two pairs of socks and gloves, several thin sweaters and a snow suit on top. Catching the fish is easy,' he says. 'First you break the ice and make a small round hole in it. Next you take a fishing line and put some bread on it. Then you put the line through the hole and into the water. You pull the line up when the fish eat the bread. They are between ten and twenty centimetres long. Some people like to eat them, but when I have caught three or four fish, I prefer to have some chocolate or other snack! Today I have caught twenty-five! It's a great sport and you can meet some nice people here!'

Example:

0   People can travel to Lake Nipissing by car.

   A   Right   **B**   Wrong   **C**   Doesn't say   *Answer:* | 0 | A ■ B ☐ C ☐ |

---

21   Fishermen only use the houses on Lake Nipissing in winter.

   A   Right   **B**   Wrong   **C**   Doesn't say

22   The fishermen sit in boats to catch the fish.

   A   Right   **B**   Wrong   **C**   Doesn't say

23   Bob goes to Lake Nipissing every winter.

   A   Right   **B**   Wrong   **C**   Doesn't say

24   Bob wears old clothes for ice-fishing.

   A   Right   **B**   Wrong   **C**   Doesn't say

25   The fish are usually longer than twenty centimetres.

   A   Right   **B**   Wrong   **C**   Doesn't say

26   When Bob has caught a few fish, he cooks them and eats them.

   A   Right   **B**   Wrong   **C**   Doesn't say

27   Bob thinks ice-fishing is a way of making new friends.

   A   Right   **B**   Wrong   **C**   Doesn't say

PART 5

QUESTIONS 28–35

Read the article about farming.

Choose the best word (A, B or C) for each space.

For questions 28–35, mark A, B or C on your answer sheet.

The History of Farming

Before people started farming, they went to the forest to look **(0)** .... plants or fruit they could eat. This meant that people **(28)** .... moving all the time to find food. But about 12,000 years ago, in the Middle East, people **(29)** .... to grow food. These people were the first farmers. Farming made **(30)** .... possible for people to stay in **(31)** .... place and slowly their villages got bigger.

Some people in the villages became free to do other work, like making clothes, **(32)** .... the farmers could grow food for everyone. Unfortunately, farming was difficult when the weather was bad and then some people did not get **(33)** .... food to eat.

Today, farmers **(34)** .... grow more food and it travels thousands of kilometres from where it **(35)** .... grown to our homes.

Example:

| 0 | **A** at | **B** on | **C** for | *Answer:* | 0 | A B C □□■ |

| 28 | **A** was | **B** been | **C** were |

| 29 | **A** began | **B** begin | **C** begun |

| 30 | **A** this | **B** it | **C** them |

| 31 | **A** one | **B** the | **C** other |

| 32 | **A** but | **B** or | **C** because |

| 33 | **A** enough | **B** all | **C** many |

| 34 | **A** need | **B** can | **C** have |

| 35 | **A** be | **B** being | **C** is |

PART 6

QUESTIONS 36–40

Read the descriptions of some holiday words.
What is the word for each one?
The first letter is already there. There is one space for each other letter in the word.
For questions 36–40, write the words on your answer sheet.

Example:

0 You will need to buy this to travel on a bus or an aeroplane.   t __ __ __ __ __

Answer: | **0** | *t i c k e t*

---

36 You may need to show this when you travel to a foreign country.   p __ __ __ __ __ __ __

37 The pictures you take with this will help you remember your holiday.   c __ __ __ __ __ __

38 You can sit on this on the beach or use it to dry yourself.   t __ __ __ __ __

39 Make sure this is big enough to hold all your clothes for your holiday.   s __ __ __ __ __ __ __

40 It's good to read this on the beach or in an aeroplane.   m __ __ __ __ __ __ __

PART 7

QUESTIONS 41–50

Complete the letter.

Write ONE word for each space.

For questions 41–50, write the words on your answer sheet.

Example: | **0** | *would* |

> 23 Oak Avenue
> Manchester

Dear Sir or Madam,

I **(0)** .... like a room at your hotel **(41)** .... three nights from September 15th **(42)** .... 17th.

I'd like a single room **(43)** .... a shower. I also need **(44)** .... telephone in my room. Please can I **(45)** .... a quiet room on **(46)** .... ground floor?

I am going to drive to the hotel. Is **(47)** .... a hotel car park?

I **(48)** .... arrive at about 10.30 p.m. What **(49)** .... does the restaurant close in the evening? If possible, I would like a meal **(50)** .... I arrive.

Thank you for your help.

Yours faithfully,

Mark Jones

PART 8

QUESTIONS 51–55

Read the note and the information about language classes.

Fill in the information on the registration form.

For questions 51–55, write the information on your answer sheet.

To: Anna Dahlin

Here is the information about language classes at City College. The Russian class is full and so is the German one, but there are still places in the Italian one. Please send me your registration form tomorrow.

Elaine Smith
10.06.04

Monday	**Russian**	**7 pm – 8 pm**
Tuesday	**Italian**	**6 pm – 8 pm**
Thursday	**German**	**8 pm – 9 pm**

One-hour classes: £120
Two-hour classes: £180

CITY COLLEGE
Registration Form (Language Classes)

Date: *11 June 2004*

Name of student: **51**

Language course: **52**

Day: **53**

Start time: **54**

Price: **55**

PART 9

QUESTION 56

You've just had a birthday. Write a postcard to your American friend about your favourite birthday present.

Say:

- **what** the present is
- **who** gave it to you
- **why** you like it.

Write 25–35 words.
Write the postcard on your answer sheet.

PAPER 2   LISTENING (approximately 30 minutes including 8 minutes transfer time)

PART 1

QUESTIONS 1–5

You will hear five short conversations.

You will hear each conversation twice.

There is one question for each conversation.

For questions 1–5, put a tick (✔) under the right answer.

Example:

0   How many people were at the meeting?

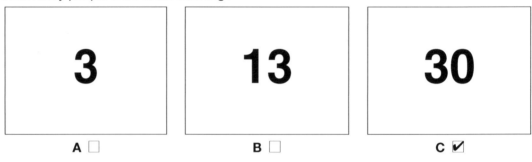

A ☐   B ☐   C ✔

---

1   What's George doing now?

A ☐   B ☐   C ☐

2   Which room will the woman stay in?

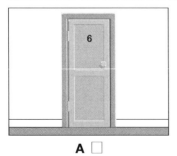 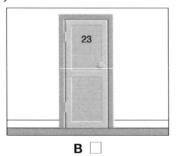 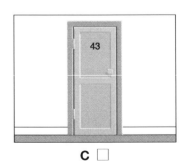

A ☐   B ☐   C ☐

3   What will the boy wear in the race?

A ☐

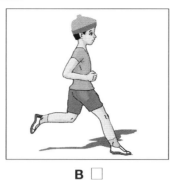

B ☐

C ☐

4   What colour will the room be?

A ☐

B ☐

C ☐

5   Where did Minnie and Richard first meet?

A ☐

B ☐

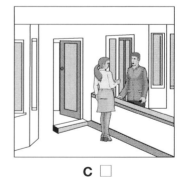

C ☐

PART 2

QUESTIONS 6–10

Listen to Jack and Mark talking about a new sports centre.
Which sport can they do each day at the centre?
For questions 6–10, write a letter A–H next to each day.
You will hear the conversation twice.

Example:

0   Monday | D |

Days

6   Tuesday

7   Wednesday

8   Thursday

9   Friday

10   Saturday

Sports

A   badminton

B   basketball

C   football

D   golf

E   hockey

F   swimming

G   tennis

H   volleyball

PART 3

QUESTIONS 11–15

Listen to Diane talking to a friend about a trip to London.
For questions 11–15, tick (✔) A, B or C.
You will hear the conversation twice.

Example:

0	Diane went to London yesterday	**A**	morning.	☐
		B	afternoon.	☐
		C	evening.	✔

11	Diane went to London by	**A**	car.	☐
		B	bus.	☐
		C	underground.	☐
12	Diane and her friends ate	**A**	Mexican food.	☐
		B	Chinese food.	☐
		C	Spanish food.	☐
13	Diane says the restaurant was	**A**	full.	☐
		B	expensive.	☐
		C	quiet.	☐

14 After the meal, Diane and her friends
    A sat and talked. ☐

    B saw a film. ☐

    C walked by the water. ☐

15 During Diane's trip to London,
    A it rained. ☐

    B it snowed. ☐

    C it was windy. ☐

PART 4

QUESTIONS 16–20

You will hear a woman talking to a shop assistant about buying a video film for her daughter.

Listen and complete questions 16–20.

You will hear the conversation twice.

VIDEO

Actor in film: Brad Smith

Name of film: **16** Blue ....

For people: **17** .... years old or more.

Cost: **18** £

Video shop in: **19** ....Street

Opposite: **20**

PART 5

QUESTIONS 21–25

You will hear some information about a visitor to a school.

Listen and complete questions 21–25.

You will hear the information twice.

BLACKBURN SCHOOL
Visiting Speaker

Day:	Thursday
Name:	**21** Dr Robert ....
Subject:	**22** Space ....
Place:	**23** School ....
Time of talk:	**24** .... p.m.
Tickets for parents cost:	**25** £

You now have 8 minutes to write your answers on the answer sheet.

PAPER 3   SPEAKING (8–10 minutes)

The Speaking test lasts 8 to 10 minutes. You will take the test with another candidate. There are two examiners, but only one of them will talk to you. The examiner will ask you questions and ask you to talk to the other candidate.

Part 1 (5–6 minutes)

The examiner will ask you and your partner some questions. These questions will be about your daily life, past experience and future plans. For example, you may have to speak about your school, job, hobbies or home town.

Part 2 (3–4 minutes)

You and your partner will speak to each other. You will ask and answer questions. The examiner will give you a card with some information on it. The examiner will give your partner a card with some words on it. Your partner will use the words on the card to ask you questions about the information you have. Then you will change roles.

Test 4

PAPER 1 READING AND WRITING (1 hour 10 minutes)

PART 1

QUESTIONS 1–5

Which notice (A–H) says this (1–5)?
For questions 1–5, mark the correct letter A–H on your answer sheet.

Example:

0 For cheaper tickets, travel from Monday to Friday. *Answer:*

0	A B **C** D E F G H

---

1 You can listen to a writer here one evening this week.

A
> **STUDENT LIBRARY**
> Return books to shelves after use

B
> **All flights half price**
> **(weekdays only)**

2 If you have lost a book, call this number.

C
> **THURSDAY 8 PM**
> **MARTIN BANKS WILL READ FROM HIS LATEST BOOK**

D
> *Only take small bags into the library*

3 Always keep your bags with you.

E
> LANGUAGE CLUB
> English Conversation: 1–2 pm Fridays
> — Bring sandwiches! —

F
> *Dictionary found. Phone Simon on 529164 to get it back.*

4 When you have finished reading, put back all the books.

G
> **CITY AIRPORT**
> DO NOT LEAVE YOUR LUGGAGE UNATTENDED

5 You can eat lunch during this meeting.

H
> **CONCERT TICKET OFFICE**
> **CLOSED FOR LUNCH**
> **24-HOUR BOOKING LINE: 0845 388420**

PART 2

QUESTIONS 6–10

Read the sentences about going to a concert.
Choose the best word (A, B or C) for each space.
For questions 6–10, mark A, B or C on your answer sheet.

Example:

0 I .... to a pop concert with some friends last Friday.

   A   went   **B**   watched   **C**   saw   *Answer:*

0	A	B	C
	■	☐	☐

---

6 I finished my classes at 5 and went home to .... ready for the concert.

   A   get   **B**   come   **C**   put

7 I spent half an hour .... for the tickets.

   A   finding   **B**   keeping   **C**   looking

8 The concert started at 8 and I didn't want to arrive .... for the first band.

   A   slowly   **B**   late   **C**   soon

9 The music was very .... so I had to shout to my friends.

   A   loud   **B**   bright   **C**   strong

10 I .... an excellent time at the concert.

   A   had   **B**   made   **C**   did

PART 3

QUESTIONS 11–15

Complete the five conversations.

For questions 11–15, mark A, B or C on your answer sheet.

Example:

0

Where do you come from?

A New York.

B School.

C Home.

Answer: | 0 | A B C ■□□

---

11 I don't think I can come to the concert.

    A What time will you arrive?

    B Are you sure you can't?

    C Do you think you can?

12 Let's have supper now.

    A You aren't eating.

    B There aren't any.

    C Bill isn't here yet.

13 Have you shut the windows?

    A I'll just check.

    B You don't remember.

    C It isn't open.

14 My street is too noisy.

    A That's a pity!

    B Do you like it?

    C Be careful!

15 Can I speak to John, please?

    A Speaking.

    B It doesn't matter.

    C How are you?

QUESTIONS 16–20

Complete the conversation between two friends.

What does Helen say to Amy?

For questions 16–20, mark the correct letter A–H on your answer sheet.

Example:

Amy: Helen, you went to university, didn't you?
Can I ask you something?

Helen: **0** ....

Answer: **0** [A B **C** D E F G H]

Amy: I can't decide what subject to study at university.

Helen: **16** ....

Amy: I always do well in chemistry exams.

Helen: **17** ....

Amy: I don't agree. I don't like it. What I really enjoy studying is history.

Helen: **18** ....

Amy: Yes. They all say I should choose the subject I enjoy the most.

Helen: **19** ....

Amy: Well, Dad wants me to do business studies so I can earn a lot like you!

Helen: **20** ....

Amy: So I should choose history then!

A I don't like history much.

B What about your parents?

C Of course you can. What's the problem?

D Well, that's an interesting and useful science subject.

E Where will you study?

F I agree, money is quite important but I think your teachers are right.

G Have you talked to your teachers about it?

H Which subject are you best at?

PART 4

QUESTIONS 21–27

Read the article about Corryvale Farm.

Are sentences 21–27 'Right' (A) or 'Wrong' (B)?

If there is not enough information to answer 'Right' (A) or 'Wrong' (B), choose 'Doesn't say' (C).

For questions 21–27, mark A, B or C on your answer sheet.

Corryvale Farm

Corryvale Farm is in the west of England. Stephen and Jenny Blackler keep cows and chickens and sell milk and eggs. But most of their money comes from Jenny's sheep.

She has 50 sheep and each one has enough wool for six sweaters. Every six months, Stephen cuts this wool off the sheep so they won't get too warm. Five years ago, Jenny made some sweaters with the wool and tried to sell them at country markets. But it was summer and the weather was hot so people didn't want to buy sweaters. She then made some socks. Everybody loved them because they were cheap, strong and easy to wash.

That's how Jenny's business started. At first she made the socks at home, but soon she had thousands of customers so she had to send the wool to a factory, where all the socks are now made on machines. There are six colours, five sizes for all ages, and different socks for walkers, sportsmen and skiers. Jenny is busiest at Christmas because Corryvale socks are a favourite present. On the walls of Jenny's office, there are lots of letters from happy customers all over the world.

Example:

0   The Blacklers earn more from their sheep than from their other animals.

   A   Right   **B**   Wrong   **C**   Doesn't say   *Answer:*   **0**   [A ■] [B ☐] [C ☐]

---

21   Jenny only gets wool from her sheep once a year.

   A   Right   **B**   Wrong   **C**   Doesn't say

22   It took Jenny a long time to make the sweaters.

   A   Right   **B**   Wrong   **C**   Doesn't say

23   Jenny couldn't sell the sweaters because it was the wrong time of year.

   A   Right   **B**   Wrong   **C**   Doesn't say

24   Jenny decided that socks were easier to make than sweaters.

   A   Right   **B**   Wrong   **C**   Doesn't say

25   Corryvale socks are still made on the farm.

   A   Right   **B**   Wrong   **C**   Doesn't say

26   You can't buy Corryvale socks for children.

   A   Right   **B**   Wrong   **C**   Doesn't say

27   People from many different countries buy Corryvale socks.

   A   Right   **B**   Wrong   **C**   Doesn't say

PART 5

QUESTIONS 28–35

Read the article about the Globe Theatre.

Choose the best word (A, B or C) for each space.

For questions 28–35, mark A, B or C on your answer sheet.

The Globe Theatre

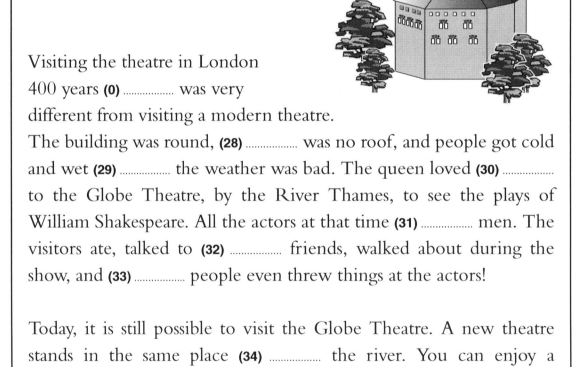

Visiting the theatre in London 400 years **(0)** .... was very different from visiting a modern theatre. The building was round, **(28)** .... was no roof, and people got cold and wet **(29)** .... the weather was bad. The queen loved **(30)** .... to the Globe Theatre, by the River Thames, to see the plays of William Shakespeare. All the actors at that time **(31)** .... men. The visitors ate, talked to **(32)** .... friends, walked about during the show, and **(33)** .... people even threw things at the actors!

Today, it is still possible to visit the Globe Theatre. A new theatre stands in the same place **(34)** .... the river. You can enjoy a Shakespeare play there or just learn **(35)** .... life in the seventeenth century.

Example:

| 0 | **A** after | **B** ago | **C** since | *Answer:* |

| 0 | A B C |

28   **A**   there   **B**   here   **C**   it

29   **A**   that   **B**   if   **C**   so

30   **A**   go   **B**   going   **C**   went

31   **A**   were   **B**   was   **C**   are

32   **A**   those   **B**   his   **C**   their

33   **A**   any   **B**   every   **C**   some

34   **A**   near   **B**   next   **C**   at

35   **A**   to   **B**   for   **C**   about

PART 6

QUESTIONS 36–40

Read the descriptions of some food and drink words.
What is the word for each one?
The first letter is already there. There is one space for each other letter in the word.
For questions 36–40, write the words on your answer sheet.

Example:

0 You need this to cut up meat.   **k** __ __ __ __

	Answer:	**0**	*k n i f e*

---

36 Soup is usually put in this.   **b** __ __ __

37 A carrot or an onion is an example of this.   **v** __ __ __ __ __ __ __ __

38 If you eat in a restaurant, this person brings your food   **w** __ __ __ __ __ __
to you.

39 You can drink the juice of this yellow fruit, but it isn't sweet.   **l** __ __ __ __

40 To make chips, you cut up potatoes, put them in oil and   **f** __ __
do this.

PART 7

QUESTIONS 41–50

Complete this letter.
Write ONE word for each space.
For questions 41–50, write the words on your answer sheet.

Example:

0	in

Dear Jeff,

I'm having a good holiday **(0)** .... Australia. When we arrived
two weeks **(41)** .... the weather was bad and **(42)** .... was
cold. Now the weather is better and we go to the beach **(43)** ....
day.

This week we **(44)** .... staying in Sydney but **(45)** .... week we
went to the Great Barrier Reef. Because **(46)** .... water was so
warm, I loved swimming there. The fish were all different
(47) .... : red, yellow, purple! Australia **(48)** .... very
beautiful. We don't want **(49)** .... come home!

See you at the end **(50)** .... September.

Sue

PART 8

QUESTIONS 51–55

Read the advertisement for a book and the e-mail.

Fill in the information on the order form.

For questions 51–55, write the information on your answer sheet.

A BOY'S LIFE
by
Mick Blake

Photos by
Chris Swan

£12.99

NEW

| To: | Ron Baker |
| From: | Jane Usher |

Can you get Mick Blake's new book for me? I think it costs £15. I can't remember what it's called. I liked his other book, 'Football Families'.

I'm going to go on holiday on 20th December so I want it by the 19th.

If there's a problem, phone me at work (922769) or in the evening, at home (765541).

Thanks.

Jane Usher

BOOK ORDER FORM

Customer's name: *Jane Usher*

Daytime phone number: **51**

Name of book: **52**

Name of writer: **53**

Price: **54** £

Date needed by: **55**

PART 9

QUESTION 56

Read this note from your friend, Ally.

Sorry I couldn't come to your birthday party.

What did you do at the party? Who was there? What presents did you get?

Ally

Write a note to Ally and answer her questions.

Write 25–35 words.

Write the note on your answer sheet.

PAPER 2 LISTENING (approximately 30 minutes including 8 minutes transfer time)

PART 1

QUESTIONS 1–5

You will hear five short conversations.

You will hear each conversation twice.

There is one question for each conversation.

For questions 1–5, put a tick (✔) under the right answer.

Example:

0   How many people were at the meeting?

3	**13**	**30**
A ☐	B ☐	C ✔

---

1   How much is the car?

£1000	£2000	£3000
A ☐	B ☐	C ☐

2   What's Elena going to take to the party?

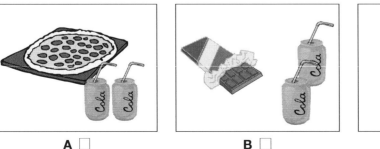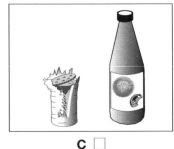

| A ☐ | B ☐ | C ☐ |

3   Where will Susan buy her eggs?

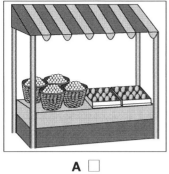

A ☐

B ☐

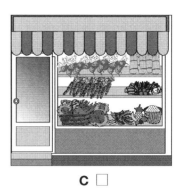

C ☐

4   What time does the film begin?

A ☐

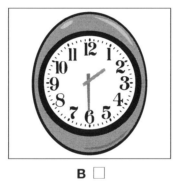

B ☐

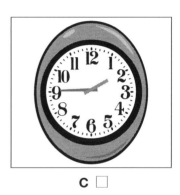

C ☐

5   How will the man travel to London?

A ☐

B ☐

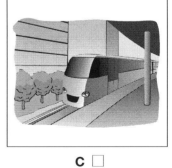

C ☐

PART 2

QUESTIONS 6–10

Listen to Sarah talking to a friend about a sports centre.
What is the problem with the different things at the sports centre?
For questions 6–10, write a letter A–H next to each thing.
You will hear the conversation twice.

Example:

0   T-shirt | **A** |

Things

6   swimming pool

7   car park

8   café

9   football club

10   tennis lessons

Problems

A   big

B   cold

C   dirty

D   expensive

E   hot

F   late

G   noisy

H   small

PART 3

QUESTIONS 11–15

Listen to Philip talking to a friend about his photography course.
For questions 11–15, tick (✔) A, B or C.
You will hear the conversation twice.

Example:

0	Where does Philip do the photography classes?	A	Park College	☐
		B	City College	✔
		C	South College	☐

11	What time do the photography classes begin?	A	5.15 p.m.	☐
		B	6.00 p.m.	☐
		C	6.45 p.m.	☐

12	How much does Philip pay for the photography course?	A	£55	☐
		B	£75	☐
		C	£95	☐

13	Philip's happy with the course because he's	A	learning about famous photographers.	☐
		B	using a new camera.	☐
		C	getting better at photography.	☐

14 Philip thinks it's easy to take photographs of

    A trees. ☐

    B animals. ☐

    C children. ☐

15 After the course, Philip will

    A buy a new camera. ☐

    B get a job in photography. ☐

    C make photography his hobby. ☐

PART 4

QUESTIONS 16–20

You will hear a man asking for information about the **Westwood English School.**
Listen and complete questions 16–20.
You will hear the conversation twice.

WESTWOOD ENGLISH SCHOOL

Evening classes on:	Thursday
Next course starts on:	**16** 22 ....
Speaking class with:	**17** Miss ....
Cost for 12 classes:	**18** £
Address:	**19** .... Fitzroy Square
School is next to the:	**20**

PART 5

QUESTIONS 21–25

You will hear some information about Finchester Zoo.

Listen and complete questions 21–25.

You will hear the information twice.

Finchester Zoo

Closed on: Monday

Closing time in summer: **21** .... p.m.

Meeting place for tour: **22**

At 2 p.m., see: **23** .... eat their food.

Zoo shop sells: **24** books and ....

Child's ticket costs: **25** £

You now have 8 minutes to write your answers on the answer sheet.

PAPER 3   SPEAKING (8–10 minutes)

The Speaking test lasts 8 to 10 minutes. You will take the test with another candidate. There are two examiners, but only one of them will talk to you. The examiner will ask you questions and ask you to talk to the other candidate.

Part 1 (5–6 minutes)

The examiner will ask you and your partner some questions. These questions will be about your daily life, past experience and future plans. For example, you may have to speak about your school, job, hobbies or home town.

Part 2 (3–4 minutes)

You and your partner will speak to each other. You will ask and answer questions. The examiner will give you a card with some information on it. The examiner will give your partner a card with some words on it. Your partner will use the words on the card to ask you questions about the information you have. Then you will change roles.

Visual materials for Paper 3

1A

NEW WORLD MUSIC SHOP

All CDs £8

Buy the latest dance music here!

Monday to Saturday 9 am – 8 pm

Books and magazines

— 58 Walton Street —

2B

CASTLE

- open / afternoon?

- student ticket? £?

- car park?

- buy / guidebook?

- telephone number?

3A

ALISON'S ANIMAL HOSPITAL

44 North Road

Help for *all* animals

7 days a week — 8 am to 5 pm

♦ **For appointments: 234567** ♦

Car park behind hospital

4B

NEW TEACHER

♦ **name?**

♦ **what / teach?**

♦ **where / from?**

♦ **when / start?**

♦ **play sport?**

1B

MUSIC SHOP

♦ **name?**

♦ **price / CDs? £?**

♦ **address?**

♦ **open / evenings?**

♦ **music magazines?**

2A

BOSTON CASTLE

** *King Alfred lived here* **

Adults: £3   Students: £2   Children: £1.50
Monday – Saturday, 10 am – 4 pm

Castle Shop – postcards, guidebooks, maps

Free Parking

For information tel: **543876**

3B

ANIMAL HOSPITAL

- ◆ **name / animal hospital?**

- ◆ **open / Sunday?**

- ◆ **for birds?**

- ◆ **address?**

- ◆ **car park?**

4A

I.C.C. College

From next Monday, our new

English and French teacher is

MR TOM COOPER

from Canada

He wants to have a football club after school.

1C

GUITAR LESSONS

Learn in your home

7 days a week – morning, afternoon or evening

All kinds of music

£90 for 10 lessons

Children from 8 years old

2D

COMPUTER CAFÉ

♦ **name / café?**

♦ **where?**

♦ **open / Sunday?**

♦ **cost? £?**

♦ **what / food?**

3C

HORSE-RIDING LESSONS

Bell Riding School
West Road

£15 per hour
Friendly, quiet horses
Classes every day

Everyone must wear a riding hat.

4D

LIBRARY

♦ where?

♦ opening times?

♦ CDs?

♦ free?

♦ computers?

1D

GUITAR LESSONS

- ◆ **cost? £?**

- ◆ **pop music?**

- ◆ **children's lessons?**

- ◆ **where?**

- ◆ **Saturday afternoon?**

2C

SMALL WORLD COMPUTER CAFÉ

£1 for 30 minutes on computer

Tuesday – Sunday 8 am – 8 pm

cakes, cold drinks, coffee

23 GEORGE STREET

3D

HORSE-RIDING LESSONS

- ◆ where?

- ◆ expensive?

- ◆ wear special clothes?

- ◆ lessons / Friday?

- ◆ nice horses?

4C

CENTRAL LIBRARY

— ◆ ◆ ◆ —

books, videos, music CDs

Videos – £1 per week

Monday – Saturday 9.30 am – 5 pm

12 computers on 4th floor

Next to City Museum

Paper 3 frames

Test 1

Note: The visual material for Paper 3 appears on pages 88–95.

Part 1 (5–6 minutes)

Greetings and introductions

At the beginning of Part 1, the interlocutor greets the candidates, asks for their names and asks them to spell something.

Giving information about place of origin, occupation, studies

The interlocutor asks the candidates about where they come from/live, and for information about their school/studies/work.

Giving general information about self

The interlocutor asks the candidates questions about their daily life, past experience or future plans. They may be asked, for example, about their likes and dislikes or about recent past experiences, or to describe and compare places.

Extended response

In the final section of Part 1, candidates are expected to give an extended response to a 'Tell me something about …' prompt. The topics are still of a personal and concrete nature. Candidates should produce at least three utterances in their extended response.

Part 2 (3–4) minutes

The interlocutor introduces the activity as follows:

Interlocutor: (*Pablo*), here is some information about a music shop.

(*Interlocutor shows answer card 1A on page 88 to Pablo.*)

(*Laura*), you don't know anything about the music shop, so ask (*Pablo*) some questions about it.

(*Interlocutor shows question card 1B on page 90 to Laura.*)

Use these words to help you. (*Interlocutor indicates prompt words.*)

Do you understand?

Now, (*Laura*), ask (*Pablo*) your questions about the music shop, and (*Pablo*), you answer them.

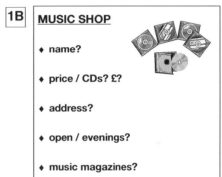

When the candidates have asked and answered their questions about the music shop, they then exchange roles and talk about a different topic.

The interlocutor introduces the activity as follows:

Interlocutor: (*Laura*), here is some information about guitar lessons.

(*Interlocutor shows answer card 1C on page 92 to Laura.*)

(*Pablo*), you don't know anything about the guitar lessons, so ask (*Laura*) some questions about them.

(*Interlocutor shows question card 1D on page 94 to Pablo.*)

Use these words to help you. (*Interlocutor indicates prompt words.*)

Do you understand?

Now, (*Pablo*), ask (*Laura*) your questions about the guitar lessons, and (*Laura*), you answer them.

Note: Candidates are assessed on both their questions and answers in Part 2 of the test.

1C
GUITAR LESSONS
Learn in your home

7 days a week – morning, afternoon or evening
All kinds of music
£90 for 10 lessons
Children from 8 years old

1D **GUITAR LESSONS**

♦ **cost? £?**

♦ **pop music?**

♦ **children's lessons?**

♦ **where?**

♦ **Saturday afternoon?**

Test 2

Note: The visual material for Paper 3 appears on pages 88–95.

Part 1 (5–6 minutes)

Greetings and introductions

At the beginning of Part 1, the interlocutor greets the candidates, asks for their names and asks them to spell something.

Giving information about place of origin, occupation, studies

The interlocutor asks the candidates about where they come from/live, and for information about their school/studies/work.

Giving general information about self

The interlocutor asks the candidates questions about their daily life, past experience or future plans. They may be asked, for example, about their likes and dislikes or about recent past experiences, or to describe and compare places.

Extended response

In the final section of Part 1, candidates are expected to give an extended response to a 'Tell me something about …' prompt. The topics are still of a personal and concrete nature. Candidates should produce at least three utterances in their extended response.

Part 2 (3–4) minutes

The interlocutor introduces the activity as follows:

Interlocutor: (*Pablo*), here is some information about a castle.

(*Interlocutor shows answer card 2A on page 90 to Pablo.*)

(*Laura*), you don't know anything about the castle, so ask (*Pablo*) some questions about it.

(*Interlocutor shows question card 2B on page 88 to Laura.*)

Use these words to help you. (*Interlocutor indicates prompt words.*)

Do you understand?

Now, (*Laura*), ask (*Pablo*) your questions about the castle, and (*Pablo*), you answer them.

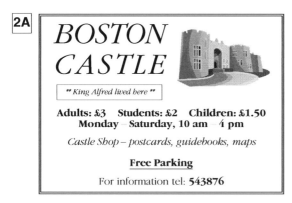

When the candidates have asked and answered their questions about the castle, they then exchange roles and talk about a different topic.

The interlocutor introduces the activity as follows:

Interlocutor: (*Laura*), here is some information about a computer café.

(*Interlocutor shows answer card 2C on page 94 to Laura.*)

(*Pablo*), you don't know anything about the computer café, so ask (*Laura*) some questions about it.

(*Interlocutor shows question card 2D on page 92 to Pablo.*)

Use these words to help you. (*Interlocutor indicates prompt words.*)

Do you understand?

Now, (*Pablo*), ask (*Laura*) your questions about the computer café, and (*Laura*), you answer them.

Note: Candidates are assessed on both their questions and answers in Part 2 of the test.

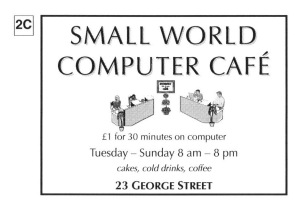

2C

SMALL WORLD COMPUTER CAFÉ

£1 for 30 minutes on computer

Tuesday – Sunday 8 am – 8 pm

cakes, cold drinks, coffee

23 GEORGE STREET

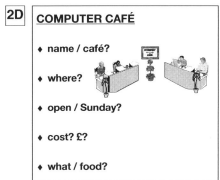

2D

COMPUTER CAFÉ

♦ **name / café?**

♦ **where?**

♦ **open / Sunday?**

♦ **cost? £?**

♦ **what / food?**

Test 3

Note: The visual material for Paper 3 appears on pages 88–95.

Part 1 (5–6 minutes)

Greetings and introductions

At the beginning of Part 1, the interlocutor greets the candidates, asks for their names and asks them to spell something.

Giving information about place of origin, occupation, studies

The interlocutor asks the candidates about where they come from/live, and for information about their school/studies/work.

Giving general information about self

The interlocutor asks the candidates questions about their daily life, past experience or future plans. They may be asked, for example, about their likes and dislikes or about recent past experiences, or to describe and compare places.

Extended response

In the final section of Part 1, candidates are expected to give an extended response to a 'Tell me something about …' prompt. The topics are still of a personal and concrete nature. Candidates should produce at least three utterances in their extended response.

Part 2 (3–4) minutes

The interlocutor introduces the activity as follows:

Interlocutor: (*Pablo*), here is some information about an animal hospital.

(*Interlocutor shows answer card 3A on page 89 to Pablo.*)

(*Laura*), you don't know anything about the animal hospital, so ask (*Pablo*) some questions about it.

(*Interlocutor shows question card 3B on page 91 to Laura.*)

Use these words to help you. (*Interlocutor indicates prompt words.*)

Do you understand?

Now, (*Laura*), ask (*Pablo*) your questions about the animal hospital, and (*Pablo*), you answer them.

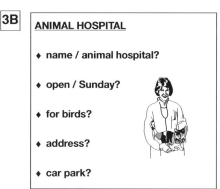

When the candidates have asked and answered their questions about the animal hospital, they then exchange roles and talk about a different topic.

The interlocutor introduces the activity as follows:

Interlocutor: (*Laura*), here is some information about some horse-riding lessons.

(*Interlocutor shows answer card 3C on page 93 to Laura.*)

(*Pablo*), you don't know anything about the horse-riding lessons, so ask (*Laura*) some questions about them.

(*Interlocutor shows question card 3D on page 95 to Pablo.*)

Use these words to help you. (*Interlocutor indicates prompt words.*)

Do you understand?

Now, (*Pablo*), ask (*Laura*) your questions about the horse-riding lessons, and (*Laura*), you answer them.

Note: Candidates are assessed on both their questions and answers in Part 2 of the test.

3C

HORSE-RIDING LESSONS
Bell Riding School
West Road

£15 per hour
Friendly, quiet horses
Classes every day

Everyone must wear a riding hat.

3D

HORSE-RIDING LESSONS

♦ **where?**

♦ **expensive?**

♦ **wear special clothes?**

♦ **lessons / Friday?**

♦ **nice horses?**

Test 4

Note: The visual material for Paper 3 appears on pages 88–95.

Part 1 (5–6 minutes)

Greetings and introductions

At the beginning of Part 1, the interlocutor greets the candidates, asks for their names and asks them to spell something.

Giving information about place of origin, occupation, studies

The interlocutor asks the candidates about where they come from/live, and for information about their school/studies/work.

Giving general information about self

The interlocutor asks the candidates questions about their daily life, past experience or future plans. They may be asked, for example, about their likes and dislikes or about recent past experiences, or to describe and compare places.

Extended response

In the final section of Part 1, candidates are expected to give an extended response to a 'Tell me something about …' prompt. The topics are still of a personal and concrete nature. Candidates should produce at least three utterances in their extended response.

Part 2 (3–4) minutes

The interlocutor introduces the activity as follows:

Interlocutor: (*Pablo*), here is some information about a new teacher.

(*Interlocutor shows answer card 4A on page 91 to Pablo.*)

(*Laura*), you don't know anything about the new teacher, so ask (*Pablo*) some questions about him.

(*Interlocutor shows question card 4B on page 89 to Laura.*)

Use these words to help you. (*Interlocutor indicates prompt words.*)

Do you understand?

Now, (*Laura*), ask (*Pablo*) your questions about the new teacher, and (*Pablo*), you answer them.

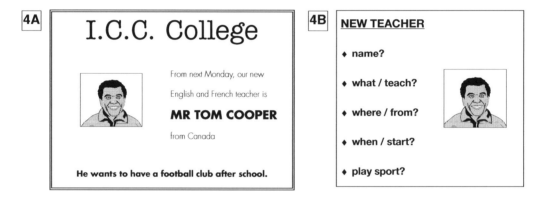

When the candidates have asked and answered their questions about the new teacher, they then exchange roles and talk about a different topic.

The interlocutor introduces the activity as follows:

Interlocutor: (*Laura*), here is some information about a library.

(*Interlocutor shows answer card 4C on page 95 to Laura.*)

(*Pablo*), you don't know anything about the library, so ask (*Laura*) some questions about it.

(*Interlocutor shows question card 4D on page 93 to Pablo.*)

Use these words to help you. (*Interlocutor indicates prompt words.*)

Do you understand?

Now, (*Pablo*), ask (*Laura*) your questions about the library, and (*Laura*), you answer them.

Note: Candidates are assessed on both their questions and answers in Part 2 of the test.

Marks and results

Paper 1   Reading and Writing

One mark is given for each correct answer in Parts 1–8. Correct spelling is required in Parts 6, 7 and 8. There are five marks for Part 9 (see below for more details). The total score of a possible 60 marks is then weighted to 50% of the marks available for the whole test.

Mark scheme for Part 9

Mark	Criteria
5	All three parts of message clearly communicated. Only minor spelling errors or occasional grammatical errors.
4	All three parts of message communicated. Some errors in spelling, grammar and/or punctuation.
3	All three parts of message attempted. Expression may require interpretation by the reader. **or** Two parts of message are clearly communicated, but one part is unattempted. Only minor spelling errors or occasional grammatical errors.
2	Only two parts of message communicated. Some errors in spelling and grammar. The errors in expression may require patience and interpretation by the reader.
1	Only one part of message communicated.
0	Question unattempted, or totally incomprehensible response.

Paper 2   Listening

One mark is given for each correct answer, making a possible total of 25, or 25% of the whole test.

Paper 3   Speaking

Throughout the Speaking test, candidates are assessed on their language skills, not their personality, intelligence or knowledge of the world. Candidates at this level are not expected to be fluent or accurate speakers, but they are expected to be able to interact and communicate appropriately according to the demands of the test. The language of the Speaking test is carefully controlled to be accessible to candidates at this level. If candidates do not understand a question or an instruction, they should ask for repetition or clarification and they will get credit for using this strategy. Similarly, they will get credit for the use of paraphrase to supplement inadequate linguistic resources. In some cases, a short response is all that is required to a question, but candidates will be given credit for extending their utterance to the phrase or sentence level, where this is appropriate. Candidates are assessed on their own individual performance and not in relation to each other, according to established criteria. In Part 2, where candidates are required to interact with each other, they will get credit for cooperating to negotiate meaning, but one candidate will not be penalised for another's shortcomings.

The marks given for the whole test are awarded on the basis of the following criteria.

Grammar and vocabulary

This refers to the ability to use vocabulary, structure and paraphrase strategies to convey meaning. Candidates at this level are only expected to have limited linguistic resources, and it is success in using these limited resources to communicate a message which is being assessed, rather than range and accuracy.

Pronunciation

This refers to the intelligibility of the candidate's speech. First language interference is expected and not penalised if it does not affect communication.

Interactive communication

This refers to the ability to take part in interaction, with the examiner and the other candidate, appropriately and with a reasonable degree of fluency. Hesitation while the candidate searches for language is expected and not penalised as long as it does not strain the patience of the listener. Candidates should also display the ability to ask for repetition or clarification, if necessary.

The Speaking test is conducted by two examiners (an interlocutor and an assessor). The assessor awards a mark out of five for each of the three criteria, while the interlocutor gives an impression mark out of five. A total mark out of 20 is weighted to give a final total out of 25.

Test 1 Key

Paper 1　Reading and Writing

Part 1

1 G　　**2** D　　**3** A　　**4** E　　**5** C

Part 2

6 B　　**7** A　　**8** B　　**9** B　　**10** C

Part 3

11 C　　**12** C　　**13** B　　**14** A　　**15** A
16 G　　**17** F　　**18** A　　**19** E　　**20** H

Part 4

21 A　　**22** A　　**23** C　　**24** B　　**25** A　　**26** C　　**27** B

Part 5

28 A　　**29** B　　**30** B　　**31** B　　**32** A　　**33** C　　**34** A　　**35** A

Part 6

For questions 36–40, spelling must be correct.

36 dictionary　　**37** magazine　　**38** diary　　**39** message　　**40** newspaper

Part 7

For questions 41–50, ignore capitals / absence of capitals. Spelling must be correct.

41 about/of　　**42** after/when/as/before　　**43** was/felt/seemed　　**44** like/love/hope
45 this/next　　**46** lot/number　　**47** have/need/ought　　**48** What/How　　**49** Are
50 one/something/it

Part 8

For questions 51–55, spelling must be correct.

51 Manchester (station)　　**52** 14 March　　**53** 12.45 / twelve forty-five / quarter to one
54 (a/my) handbag　　**55** 723419

Part 9

Question 56

The three pieces of information that must be communicated are:

i　where they will eat
ii　what time the candidate can come
iii　where Spencer can park.

Sample answer A

Mark: 5

> *Hello Spenser! We can eat in 'La Farinda' restaurant. I can come at nine oclock. You can park your car in a free car park behind of the restaurant. Kisses, Anna*

All three points are clearly and fully communicated with very minor errors.

Sample answer B

Mark: 4

> *Hey Spencer,*
> *We go to eat Taiwanes food at night maket. I think that we date five oclock at my house. and your car in front of my house. and then we go night market together.*
> *Bye Jing*

All three points are covered with some errors in grammar and spelling.

Sample answer C

Mark: 3

> *Hi Sara,*
> *It's a good idea to meet and go to a restaurant. I think we have a great time. Lets go to the new restaurant near the station. It's great! Lets go at five o'clock.*
> *Bye Mario*

This note is well written and would have scored a 5 if all three parts of the message had been included. As there are only two, it is reduced to a 3.

Sample answer D

Mark: 2

> *Dear spencer:*
> *Lets meeting near my brother hourse – is nere the restrint. I thing we can eating good food there we can meting nin past half. See you later.*
> *Zara*

The first two parts of the message are communicated but require some interpretation. The third point is not included.

Sample answer E

Mark: 0

> *Dear Spenser,*
> *How are you? I hope you are very well. I am very busi whit my school. On*
> *saturday I will go to party? Will you come with me. We can go together in*
> *my car. We can eat food there.*
> *Love Maria*

This candidate has not answered the question and so cannot be awarded any marks.

Paper 2   Listening

Part 1

1 C   **2** B   **3** B   **4** A   **5** B

Part 2

6 H   **7** B   **8** D   **9** G   **10** F

Part 3

11 B   **12** A   **13** C   **14** A   **15** B

Part 4

For questions 16–20, ignore capitals / absence of capitals. Spelling must be correct.
16 (the) April (Hotel)   **17** Leith   **18** 10.20 / ten twenty / twenty past ten
19 (the/a/Ian's) book   **20** Tuesday

Part 5

For questions 21–25, ignore capitals / absence of capitals. Spelling must be correct.
21 7.30 (p.m./pm) / 19.30 / seven thirty / half past seven (at night)   **22** North
23 3rd / (the) third (of) / 3 / 03   **24** T(-)/t(-)/tee shirts   **25** 12 / twelve (pounds)

Transcript

PART 1   *Now, look at the instructions for Part One.*

[pause]

You will hear five short conversations. You will hear each conversation twice. There is one question for each conversation. For questions 1 to 5, put a tick under the right answer.

Here is an example:
How many people were at the meeting?

Woman: Were there many people at the meeting?
Man: About thirty.
Woman: That's not many.
Man: No, but more than last time.

[pause]

The answer is 30, so there is a tick in box C.
Now we are ready to start. Look at question one.

[pause]

Question 1   *One. What music will they have at the party?*

Woman: Are you going to bring your guitar to the party?
Man: It's broken, I'm afraid. But you can play the piano for us.
Woman: I'm not good enough. Let's just play your new CDs.
Man: All right. I'll bring the guitar another time.

[pause]

Now listen again.

[repeat]

[pause]

Question 2   *Two. When will the man go on holiday?*

Man: I can't go on holiday in June because my parents are coming to stay with me then.
Woman: Why don't you go in August? It's a lovely month in the mountains.
Man: July's better. There aren't so many people, so I'll leave on the twelfth and come back at the end of the month.
Woman: OK, then you'll be back for my birthday party in August.

[pause]

Now listen again.

[repeat]

[pause]

Question 3   *Three. What will the weather be like tomorrow?*

Man: It's very hot, isn't it?
Woman: Yes, I love it. I hope it doesn't rain.
Man: Well, it'll be cold and windy tomorrow.
Woman: Oh dear, we never have hot weather for long.

[pause]

Now listen again.

[repeat]

[pause]

Question 4   *Four. What colour is Mary's coat?*

Friend: Hi, Mary. What have you bought?
Mary: This coat. Do you like it?
Friend: Yes, yellow looks good on you.
Mary: Do you think I can use my blue bag with it?
Friend: Your brown one will look better.

[pause]

Now listen again.

[repeat]

[pause]

Question 5   *Five. What did the woman repair?*

Man: Hi. What have you done today?
Woman.   You know that broken shelf above my desk? Well, I repaired it and
            then I went shopping.
Man: What did you buy?
Woman: A new chair.

[pause]

Now listen again.

[repeat]

[pause]

This is the end of Part One. Now look at Part Two.

[pause]

PART 2   *Listen to Sarah talking to a friend about her holiday photographs.*
            What place is each person in?
            For questions 6 to 10, write a letter, A to H, next to each person.
            You will hear the conversation twice.

[pause]

Sarah: I've got some photos of my holiday in Spain here.
Friend: Did you go with your family, Sarah?
Sarah: Yes. This is my mother walking in the mountains.
Friend: What lovely trees!

Sarah:	And this is my sister, Caroline, swimming. She preferred swimming here to the hotel pool.
Friend:	The sea looks very blue. And who's this standing outside a castle?
Sarah:	Jack. But it's not a castle, it's a cathedral. It's one of the oldest in Spain.
Friend:	And is this you, Sarah, buying bananas in a market?
Sarah:	Yes, that wasn't far from our hotel. The fruit was really cheap there.
Friend:	And here's Peter eating. Is he in the garden of your hotel?
Sarah:	Actually, it's a restaurant near the cathedral. We often went there.
Friend:	What's your father doing with the cassette recorder in this photo?
Sarah:	Oh. He loves history. He's in a museum here listening to information. That was his favourite day, because we also visited a castle in the morning.
Friend:	They're great photos, Sarah.

[pause]

Now listen again.

[repeat]

[pause]

This is the end of Part Two. Now look at Part Three.

[pause]

PART 3   *Listen to Sue talking to her friend, Jim, about the new sports centre.*
For questions 11 to 15, tick A, B or C. You will hear the conversation twice.
Look at questions 11 to 15 now. You have twenty seconds.

[pause]

Now listen to the conversation.

Sue:	Have you been to the new sports centre, Jim?
Jim:	Yes, Sue. It's not cheap but it's big and light.
Sue:	Does bus eighteen go there?
Jim:	That's right. It takes fifteen minutes. Don't get bus twenty-five because you have to walk a long way.
Sue:	I like doing sport early in the morning. Is it open at seven?
Jim:	Yes, you can go there from six, except on Sundays. Then it doesn't open until nine. The swimming pool has good hot showers; you have to bring your own towel but you can get soap there. They don't make you wear a swimming hat.
Sue:	Do they sell things to eat there?
Jim:	Only sandwiches; they don't sell drinks. I usually take some fruit.
Sue:	I'd love to go with you next week. How about Wednesday?
Jim:	Well, I work until late on Wednesday. I'm free on Saturday but it's too busy then. It'll have to be Thursday.
Sue:	OK. See you then.

[pause]

Now listen again.

[repeat]

[pause]

This is the end of Part Three. Now look at Part Four.

[pause]

PART 4 *You will hear a man making a telephone call.*
Listen and complete questions 16 to 20. You will hear the conversation twice.

[pause]

Ian:	Hello, could I speak to Diana, please?
Woman:	She's not in at the moment. Can I take a message?
Ian:	Yes, please. Tell her that Ian called from Head Office and we've booked her into the April Hotel for two nights.
Woman:	Which hotel?
Ian:	The April. You know, like the month.
Woman:	Oh, yes.
Ian:	I'm sure she'll like it. It's on Leith Street.
Woman:	Could you spell that?
Ian:	L E I T H. Leith Street.
Woman:	OK, I've got that.
Ian:	Now, she knows where the meeting will be, but she doesn't know the time. Tell her it will begin at twenty past ten and finish at four thirty.
Woman:	Right.
Ian:	And could you tell her to take the book with her? She'll know which one. I'm sure she's finished reading it.
Woman:	OK – anything else?
Ian:	Oh yes – please tell her I'll take her to the factory on Tuesday and she can speak to Mr Brown on Wednesday morning.
Woman:	All right, I'll make sure she gets the message.
Ian:	Thanks very much.

[pause]

Now listen again.

[repeat]

[pause]

This is the end of Part Four. Now look at Part Five.

[pause]

PART 5   *You will hear some information about a zoo.*
Listen and complete questions 21 to 25. You will hear the information twice.

[pause]

Man: Thank you for phoning Park Zoo. The zoo is open from Monday to Saturday from nine in the morning to seven thirty at night and on Sundays from ten to five. You can stay in the zoo for one hour after closing time. The zoo is north of the city centre and you should take the train to North Station. It is a five-minute walk from there.

We have many interesting animals for you to see. But please note the elephant house won't be open on the third of May. I'm sorry, but you can't see the elephants that day.

When you come, make sure you visit the zoo shop. There you can buy books, postcards and T-shirts. Everyone will want to wear a zoo T-shirt!

An adult ticket costs ten pounds, a children's ticket five pounds and a family ticket twelve pounds. We hope you enjoy your visit to the zoo.

[pause]

Now listen again.

[repeat]

[pause]

This is the end of Part Five.

You now have eight minutes to write your answers on the answer sheet.

Note: Teacher, stop the recording here and time eight minutes. Remind students when there is **one** minute remaining.

[pause]

This is the end of the test.

Test 2 Key

Paper 1 Reading and Writing

Part 1

1 E   **2** G   **3** F   **4** D   **5** B

Part 2

6 C   **7** C   **8** B   **9** C   **10** B

Part 3

11 A   **12** A   **13** C   **14** B   **15** C
16 G   **17** H   **18** A   **19** D   **20** B

Part 4

21 A   **22** C   **23** B   **24** A   **25** B   **26** A   **27** B

Part 5

28 C   **29** A   **30** C   **31** B   **32** B   **33** B   **34** A   **35** C

Part 6

For questions 36–40, spelling must be correct.

36 happy   **37** tired   **38** dirty   **39** hungry/hunger   **40** thirsty

Part 7

For questions 41–50, ignore capitals / absence of capitals. Spelling must be correct.

41 with   **42** where/anywhere   **43** there   **44** would/'d   **45** you
46 are/look/seem/sound   **47** have   **48** her/their   **49** has   **50** will/'ll

Part 8

For questions 51–55, spelling must be correct.

51 (play) tennis / go to tennis   **52** Jack   **53** Bridges Café
54 guitar / Spanish / Spanish guitar   **55** £16.50 / sixteen (pounds) (and) fifty (p/pence) / money

Part 9

Question 56

The three pieces of information that must be communicated are:

i   the candidate's age
ii   the number of the candidate's brothers and sisters, if he/she has any
iii   the candidate's favourite hobby.

Sample answer A

Mark: 5

> Dear Penfriend,
> My name is Omar and I'm 16 years. I am have three brothers and no
> sisters. My favourite hobby is playing football with my brothers.
> Omar

All three points are clearly covered with very minor errors.

Sample answer B

Mark: 4

> Hello Alex!!
> I am penfriend too. I like write to you about me. My name is José. My old
> is 14 years. I have no bother and sister. I like watch the TV. And you? Is
> the same I think.
> Write soon!!
> José

All three points are included. There are a few minor errors but none of them impede comprehension.

Sample answer C

Mark: 3

> I'm Sylvia, your new pen friend too. I have thirteen years old. My best
> hobby is play the computer games with my sister. I have one sister only.

Although all three points are clearly covered, there are some errors and as there is no opening or closing greeting in the message, one extra mark is deducted.

Sample answer D

Mark: 1

> Hallo Alex Penfiend. I very like have new penfriend. Is very good. Really I
> would like to be good penfind. I am 18 year old and I have. I find my
> favourite hooby.

Only one part of the message is attempted and the rest of the answer contains a considerable number of errors which would require patience by the reader.

Sample answer E

Mark: 0

> *Alex, I hafe some question to you. Do you like computer. How much is computer. Is computer many people in england. Please write my answer to question very soon. Fatima*

This candidate has not completed the task which was set.

Paper 2 Listening

Part 1

1 B   **2** B   **3** C   **4** C   **5** A

Part 2

6 E   **7** C   **8** H   **9** G   **10** D

Part 3

11 A   **12** B   **13** B   **14** C   **15** C

Part 4

For questions 16–20, ignore capitals / absence of capitals. Spelling must be correct.
16 Brierley   **17** (the) 9(th) / ninth (of)   **18** March
19 365 / three hundred and sixty-five (pounds)   **20** train

Part 5

For questions 21–25, ignore capitals / absence of capitals. Spelling must be correct, except in question 23, where recognisable spelling is acceptable.
21 T(-)/t(-)/tee shirt   **22** Davey(')s(')   **23** (the) cinema   **24** large
25 8.99 / eight (pounds) (and) ninety-nine (p/pence)

Transcript

This is the Cambridge Key English Test. Paper 2. Listening. Test number two. There are five parts to the test. Parts One, Two, Three, Four and Five. We will now stop for a moment before we start the test. Please ask any questions now because you mustn't speak during the test.

[pause]

PART 1   *Now, look at the instructions for Part One.*

[pause]

You will hear five short conversations. You will hear each conversation twice. There is one question for each conversation. For questions 1 to 5, put a tick under the right answer.

Here is an example:
How many people were at the meeting?

Woman: Were there many people at the meeting?
Man: About thirty.
Woman: That's not many.
Man: No, but more than last time.

[pause]

The answer is 30, so there is a tick in box C.
Now we are ready to start. Look at question one.

[pause]

Question 1   *One. What are they going to buy for Pam?*

Man: Last year we gave Pam a book for her birthday. Shall we buy her another one this year?
Woman: I think we should give her a plant or some chocolates.
Man: But she doesn't like sweet things!
Woman: Let's get her something to put in her garden, but not a book again!

[pause]

Now listen again.

[repeat]

[pause]

Question 2   *Two. When is the man's appointment?*

Man: Good morning. I'd like someone to cut my hair, please. Can I make an appointment?
Woman: Certainly. Um, Wednesday or Thursday morning, or Friday afternoon?
Man: On Friday, I'm going to go to France. What about Thursday afternoon? I'm afraid I have a meeting all day Wednesday.
Woman: Well, it's a little difficult, but if that's the only afternoon you can come, we'll see you then.

[pause]

Now listen again.

[repeat]

[pause]

Question 3 *Three. Which is the aunt's postcard?*

Boy: Look, Sandra. I got this really nice postcard from my aunt.

Sandra: Oh. What a pretty village and it's right by a river. Is it in the mountains?

Boy: Yes. But you can't see them in the picture.

Sandra: Perhaps they're behind those tall trees.

[pause]

Now listen again.

[repeat]

[pause]

Question 4 *Four. What time will the plane to Milan leave?*

Man: Excuse me. What time is the next plane to Milan?

Woman: It should leave at quarter past seven but it's an hour late today.

Man: That's a problem. If it doesn't leave until quarter past eight, I'll be one hour late for my meeting.

Woman: I'm sorry, sir. There's nothing I can do.

[pause]

Now listen again.

[repeat]

[pause]

Question 5 *Five. What does Joe's father do?*

Girl: What's your father's job, Joe?

Joe: He was a pilot but now he's a farmer. What about your father?

Girl: He's a photographer.

Joe: Oh, I want to do that – if I don't become a pilot.

[pause]

Now listen again.

[repeat]

[pause]

This is the end of Part One. Now look at Part Two.

[pause]

PART 2
Listen to Sarah and Matthew talking about the people they met at a party.
What do they say about each person?
For questions 6 to 10, write a letter, A to H, next to each person.
You will hear the conversation twice.

[pause]

Matthew:	Did you like the party, Sarah?
Sarah:	Yes, Matthew. I met a lot of people. Did you see Jenny? The girl with the short blonde hair?
Matthew:	I think so. Was she talking to John at the beginning of the evening?
Sarah:	Yes. I tried to speak to him later but he didn't say much.
Matthew:	He's OK. He just prefers not to talk a lot.
Sarah:	Who was the girl who arrived late? She was very friendly. She knew everyone.
Matthew:	That was Mary. She's certainly not quiet!
Sarah:	I know her brother, Bob. He was there too.
Matthew:	He's still at school, isn't he?
Sarah:	Yes. Everyone was a lot older than him. But he didn't mind.
Matthew:	Another person I liked was David.
Sarah:	Is he rather short?
Matthew:	Not at all. He was taller than everybody there! Who else did you meet?
Sarah:	Sally. She's travelled all over the world and knows a lot of famous people. Everything she said was interesting.
Matthew:	It was a good party.

[pause]

Now listen again.

[repeat]

[pause]

This is the end of Part Two. Now look at Part Three.

[pause]

PART 3
Listen to Anne asking her friend about going to a shopping centre.
For questions 11 to 15, tick A, B or C. You will hear the conversation twice.
Look at questions 11 to 15 now. You have twenty seconds.

[pause]

Now listen to the conversation.

Friend:	Anne, have you been to that new shopping centre?
Anne:	The Forest Centre?
Friend:	No. I mean Queen's, the new one near the river.
Anne:	Oh. I've seen the advertisement. It's got the largest café and bookshop in the country.
Friend:	It will have. Only the clothes shops are open this month.
Anne:	Well, that's OK. But it's at least thirty kilometres away and I haven't got a car.

Friend:	Well, there is a coach once a week.
Anne:	Is there? I can get that if it's not on Saturday. I have to work then.
Friend:	It goes on Tuesday. But it's best to get your ticket on Monday.
Anne:	Is the ticket expensive?
Friend:	Ten pounds eighty for adults, two pounds fifty for children and only five pounds sixty for students like you.
Anne:	Not bad. Does it go from the bus station?
Friend:	Yes, and it stops in Market Square and outside the museum in Broad Street.
Anne:	Oh, good. I'll get it there. Broad Street is really near my house. Does it leave early?
Friend:	Twenty past nine and you get to the shopping centre forty minutes later at ten o'clock.
Anne:	Great!

[pause]

Now listen again.

[repeat]

[pause]

This is the end of Part Three. Now look at Part Four.

[pause]

PART 4   *You will hear a telephone conversation about a journey to New York.*
Listen and complete questions 16 to 20. You will hear the conversation twice.

[pause]

Woman:	Good morning. John Locke Travel Service. Can I help you?
Man:	Yes. I'd like to go to the United States, to New York.
Woman:	Certainly. Could I have your name please, sir?
Man:	Brierley. That's B R I E R L E Y.
Woman:	Thank you. Now when would you like to travel, Mr Brierley?
Man:	I have to be in New York on the eleventh of December, so I'd like to leave on the ninth. Can you do that?
Woman:	Certainly, sir, and when do you want to return?
Man:	Three and a half months later, on the thirtieth of March. I must be back here in April.
Woman:	OK. One moment, Mr Brierley. I can book that for you now.
Man:	Good. How much will it cost?
Woman:	Three hundred and sixty-five pounds – that's a special price for business travellers.
Man:	That's fine.
Woman:	Will you drive your car to the airport or go by taxi?
Man:	I'll take the train. Can you get me a ticket for that too?
Woman:	Yes, or course, sir. Can you give me your credit card number ...

[pause]

Now listen again.

[repeat]

[pause]

This is the end of Part Four. Now look at Part Five.

[pause]

PART 5   *You will hear Susanna leaving a phone message for her mother.*
Listen and complete questions 21 to 25. You will hear the information twice.

[pause]

Susanna: Hi, Mum. This is Susanna. I know you're going shopping this afternoon. Can you get something for me? I need a white T-shirt for the school tennis match tomorrow. We all have to wear white, and I haven't got one. You can get them in Davey's – that's D A V E Y S – it's a new shop in the High Street. It's not far from the car park – you can go there before you go to the supermarket. You know the cinema? Well, it's next to that. It's easy to find.
        There are three sizes – small, medium and large. My old one was a small but I'm a lot bigger now, so could you buy me a large one, please?
        I hope you can get it – I can't play in the match without it. It's not expensive, it only costs eight pounds ninety-nine. I'll give you the money tonight.
        Thanks a lot, Mum. See you later. Bye.

[pause]

Now listen again.

[repeat]

[pause]

This is the end of Part Five.

You now have eight minutes to write your answers on the answer sheet.

Note: Teacher stop the recording here and time eight minutes. Remind students when there is **one** minute remaining.

[pause]

This is the end of the test.

Test 3 Key

Paper 1   Reading and Writing

Part 1

1 C   **2** G   **3** E   **4** D   **5** A

Part 2

6 A   **7** C   **8** B   **9** C   **10** B

Part 3

11 B   **12** B   **13** C   **14** A   **15** A
16 F   **17** C   **18** A   **19** H   **20** E

Part 4

21 A   **22** B   **23** A   **24** C   **25** B   **26** B   **27** A

Part 5

28 C   **29** A   **30** B   **31** A   **32** C   **33** A   **34** B   **35** C

Part 6

For questions 36–40, spelling must be correct.

36 passport   **37** camera   **38** towel   **39** suitcase   **40** magazine

Part 7

For questions 41–50, ignore capitals / absence of capitals. Spelling must be correct.

41 for   **42** to/until/till   **43** with/and/near   **44** a/to
45 have/book/reserve/request/get/take   **46** the   **47** there   **48** will/should/shall/'ll
49 time   **50** when/after

Part 8

For questions 51–55, spelling must be correct.

51 Anna Dahlin   **52** Italian   **53** Tuesday
54 6(.00) (p.m./pm) / 18.00 / six o'clock (in the evening)
55 £180 / one hundred and eighty pounds

Part 9

Question 56

The three pieces of information that must be communicated are:

i   what the present is
ii   who gave it to the candidate
iii   why the candidate likes it.

Sample answer A

Mark: 5

> Hello my dear friend,
> I want you to know I have finished my birthday. I have a motorbike
> present. My brother buy me the motorbike. Do you know, I like it so much
> because I want to race with the other motorbikes. Okay. See you soon
> Bye.

A full answer, covering all points in the question.

Sample answer B

Mark: 4

> Hi Kriya,
> It was my birthday for two weeks ago and i get a very nice present and
> the best present i liked was the ring my boyfriend gaved to me the why i
> liked the ring it because it was so beautiful. from Nasra.

All points required are answered but there are some errors in spelling, punctuation
and grammar.

Sample answer C

Mark: 3

> Dear Mohamme,
> I've just had a birthday last Saturday. The best thing I've never received
> in my life like gift which was a car. My father gave to me. I am really
> excited.
> I'll write soon,
> Your best friend ROMAINE

Two points are clearly covered here but we do not know why the writer liked the
present, and so the third point is not clear.

Sample answer D

Mark: 1

> *Daer Angeline,*
> *How are you? I'm fine. I'm Clara, your friend. What the present is your*
> *favourite? My favourite present in my birthday was the bicycle. Who gave*
> *it to you in this year? In this year, in my birthday had ten presents. but*
> *my favourite is bicycle. What is for you? Why you like it?*
> *One kiss, your friend Clara.*

Despite the length of the answer, only one point is covered.

Sample answer E

Mark: 0

> *Dear Mike Smith,*
> *Wath present do you like? Do you like a bike or a skate? Why do you like*
> *comics? Who gave it to you? Guillermo Gonzales 12th juni.*

The writer asks new questions here and does not answer the question at all.

Paper 2   Listening

Part 1

1 C   **2** B   **3** C   **4** A   **5** C

Part 2

6 B   **7** F   **8** C   **9** H   **10** G

Part 3

11 B   **12** B   **13** A   **14** C   **15** C

Part 4

For questions 16–20, ignore capitals / absence of capitals. Spelling must be correct, except in question 16, where recognisable spelling is acceptable.

16 Café   **17** 12 / twelve   **18** 5.99 / five (pounds) (and) ninety-nine (p/pence)
19 Shirley   **20** (the) bank

Part 5

For questions 21–25, ignore capitals / absence of capitals. Spelling must be correct.

21 Teale   **22** travel   **23** hall   **24** 2.30 / 14.30 / two thirty / half past two
25 3.85 / three (pounds) (and) eighty-five (p/pence)

Transcript

This is the Cambridge Key English Test. Paper 2. Listening. Test number three. There are five parts to the test. Parts One, Two, Three, Four and Five. We will now stop for a moment before we start the test. Please ask any questions now because you mustn't speak during the test.

[pause]

PART 1   *Now, look at the instructions for Part One.*

[pause]

You will hear five short conversations. You will hear each conversation twice. There is one question for each conversation. For questions 1 to 5, put a tick under the right answer.

Here is an example:
How many people were at the meeting?

Woman:	Were there many people at the meeting?
Man:	About thirty.
Woman:	That's not many.
Man:	No, but more than last time.

[pause]

The answer is 30, so there is a tick in box C.
Now we are ready to start. Look at question one.

[pause]

Question 1   *One. What's George doing now?*

Woman:	Hi. Where's George? Is he still studying?
Man:	He's driving his girlfriend to the airport.
Woman:	Oh. Will he be back for the volleyball game?
Man:	I don't think so. We'll have to play without him.

[pause]

Now listen again.

[repeat]

[pause]

Question 2   *Two. Which room will the woman stay in?*

Man:	Here's your key, Mrs Hill. Your room is number forty-three ... up the stairs and turn right.
Mrs Hill:	Is it a quiet room?
Man:	Well, it's quieter at the back of the hotel. Here, have this one if you prefer.
Mrs Hill:	Number twenty-three. Thanks. I'll need the room for six nights.

[pause]

Now listen again.

[repeat]

[pause]

Question 3   *Three. What will the boy wear in the race?*

Woman: Have you got everything for the race?
Boy: Yes, I think so. I'll wear these long running trousers.
Woman: It's quite cold. Don't you want your hat too?
Boy: It's in my bag – I'll put it on later.

[pause]

Now listen again.

[repeat]

[pause]

Question 4   *Four. What colour will the room be?*

Boy: What colour are you going to have your room, Ann?
Ann: I'd like to paint it green but Mum thinks yellow looks warmer.
Boy: Orange is my favourite colour.
Ann: I like it too but I'll have to do what Mum wants.

[pause]

Now listen again.

[repeat]

[pause]

Question 5   *Five. Where did Minnie and Richard first meet?*

Woman: Richard, have you met the new student in our class?
Richard: Do you mean Minnie?
Woman: Yes, she's the one who's a very good tennis player.
Richard: I've known her since January – that's when her family moved next
                door to mine.

[pause]

Now listen again.

[repeat]

[pause]

This is the end of Part One. Now look at Part Two.

[pause]

PART 2   *Listen to Jack and Mark talking about a new sports centre.*
            Which sport can they do each day at the centre?
            For questions 6 to 10, write a letter, A to H, next to each day.
            You will hear the conversation twice.

[pause]

Mark: Hello, Jack. You want to go to the sports centre one day a week,
            don't you? Well, I've got some information. On Monday there's golf.
Jack: Mmm. I prefer volleyball, Mark. Also, Monday's a bad day for me.
            Tuesday's better. Is there volleyball then?

Mark:	It's basketball, but you like that, don't you?
Jack:	Quite. What can you do on Wednesday?
Mark:	Let's see. It was badminton, but not enough people wanted to do it so it's swimming now. That's no good for me because I hate water.
Jack:	And I go to swimming at school every Tuesday. Is there anything outside? Football or hockey?
Mark:	On Thursday. But they don't do hockey, I'm afraid, just football. But look, Friday is good.
Jack:	Why?
Mark:	You say you like volleyball. Well, that's at the sports centre then.
Jack:	Great.
Mark:	Or there's Saturday.
Jack:	Swimming again?
Mark:	Tennis. That's outside and you like it better than football, don't you?
Jack:	Yes, but I like volleyball best.

[pause]

Now listen again.

[repeat]

[pause]

This is the end of Part Two. Now look at Part Three.

[pause]

PART 3   *Listen to Diane talking to a friend about a trip to London.*
For questions 11 to 15, tick A, B or C. You will hear the conversation twice.
Look at questions 11 to 15 now. You have twenty seconds.

[pause]

Now listen to the conversation.

Friend:	I tried to phone you yesterday.
Diane:	Oh, sorry. I was busy all day and then I went to London in the evening for a meal with some friends.
Friend:	Did you take your car?
Diane:	I left it at home. Parking's such a problem. But the underground was closed for repairs so I had to take the bus. It was quite slow.
Friend:	Did you go to your favourite Spanish restaurant?
Diane:	I was hoping to try some Mexican food but my friends booked a table in a Chinese place.
Friend:	Was it expensive?
Diane:	Quite cheap actually, and the food was very good – but it's only a small restaurant so a lot of people had to wait for tables – and it was quite noisy.
Friend:	You didn't stay there and talk afterwards then!
Diane:	We went for a walk along the river. It was too late for the cinema.
Friend:	Didn't you get wet? It rained here all evening.
Diane:	The wind was very cold but it stayed dry.
Friend:	And then it snowed during the night!

Diane: That was after I got home. But I had a really good evening!

[pause]

Now listen again.

[repeat]

[pause]

This is the end of Part Three. Now look at Part Four.

[pause]

PART 4 *You will hear a woman talking to a shop assistant about buying a video film for her daughter.*
Listen and complete questions 16 to 20. You will hear the conversation twice.

[pause]

Man: Can I help you?
Woman: I'm looking for the new Brad Smith video about a boy who works as a waiter. My daughter wants it, but I don't know the name.
Man: Oh yes. It's called *Blue Café*.
Woman: My daughter is 13. Is she old enough to watch it?
Man: It's for anyone who is 12 or older, so she'll be OK.
Woman: I hope it's not too expensive. Some videos are nearly twenty pounds.
Man: It's five pounds ninety-nine. We're selling it at a special price today.
Woman: Great. Can I have one, please?
Man: I'm sorry. I've just sold the last one. You'll have to go to our other shop.
Woman: Oh dear. Where's that?
Man: It's in Shirley Street. That's S H I R L E Y.
Woman: Oh, that's where the post office is, isn't it?
Man: Yes, the video shop's not far from there, just across the road from the bank. It's only five minutes from here.
Woman: OK. Thanks for your help.

[pause]

Now listen again.

[repeat]

[pause]

This is the end of Part Four. Now look at Part Five.

[pause]

PART 5 *You will hear some information about a visitor to a school.*
Listen and complete questions 21 to 25. You will hear the information twice.

[pause]

Man: Now listen carefully, everybody. Here is some excellent news. Next Thursday a most interesting visitor is going to come to talk to us. He is the astronaut Dr Robert Teale, that's T E A L E. I'm sure a lot of you have heard of him. He's very famous for his journeys into space.

He's going to talk to us about space travel. Only he can tell us just what it's like to travel round the earth in a spaceship, past the moon and the stars.

The whole school is going to listen to Dr Teale. We will use the school hall because none of the classrooms will be big enough. Classes will finish at twenty past two on Thursday because the talk will start at half past. Don't be late.

If your parents would like to hear Dr Teale, we have a few extra seats. The ticket price for them will be three pounds eighty-five, but of course for students it is free.

[pause]

Now listen again.

[repeat]

[pause]

This is the end of Part Five.

You now have eight minutes to write your answers on the answer sheet.

Note: Teacher, stop the recording here and time eight minutes. Remind the students when there is **one** minute remaining.

[pause]

This is the end of the test.

Test 4 Key

Paper 1 Reading and Writing

Part 1

1 C   **2** F   **3** G   **4** A   **5** E

Part 2

6 A   **7** C   **8** B   **9** A   **10** A

Part 3

11 B   **12** C   **13** A   **14** A   **15** A
16 H   **17** D   **18** G   **19** B   **20** F

Part 4

21 B   **22** C   **23** A   **24** C   **25** B   **26** B   **27** A

Part 5

28 A   **29** B   **30** B   **31** A   **32** C   **33** C   **34** A   **35** C

Part 6

For questions 36–40, spelling must be correct.
36 bowl   **37** vegetable   **38** waiter   **39** lemon   **40** fry

Part 7

For questions 41–50, ignore capitals / absence of capitals. Spelling must be correct.
41 ago   **42** it/I   **43** every/each/all   **44** are   **45** last   **46** the   **47** colours
48 is/looks/seems   **49** to   **50** of

Part 8

For questions 51–55, spelling must be correct.
51 922769   **52** A Boy's Life   **53** Mick Blake
54 12.99 / twelve (pounds) (and) ninety-nine (p/pence)   **55** (the) 19(th) December

Part 9

Question 56
The three pieces of information that must be communicated are:

i   what the candidate did at the party
ii who was at the party
iii what presents the candidate got.

Sample answer A

Mark: 5

> Dear Ally,
> At the party I ate a pizza with my friends, Jean and Marie. We saw a film
> and that I had presents: a lot of CDs and a computer game. It was very
> good.
> Bey
> Luke

A complete answer with all three points clearly communicated.

Sample answer B

Mark: 4

> Hi Ally,
> At the parti was all our friends from our class. It was a very great taim.
> We are all dance the all evening. I got many wonderfall presents such as
> book, dless, cd and computer. But best was a car! I am very happiness.
> Bye bye Reiko

All three points are covered but there are a number of errors in grammar and spelling
which bring the mark down to a 4.

Sample answer C

Mark: 3

> Dear Ally,
> I'm sorry that you couldn't come to my party. At the party there was
> dance music and we danced all night. I prepared much things to eat and
> there was a big cake. There were my best friends Maria and Luca and my
> family. My brother played the guitar and we all sang many songs. It was a
> great time.
> Love Andrea

This is a clear, well-written, accurate answer but does not include information about
the present and so can only achieve a mark of 3.

Sample answer D

Mark: 1

> *Dear Friend,*
> *Doesn't matter you no come party. I made food for all people. Here came*
> *people. I got different present, like fone and compute. Very good.*
> *Your faitfully*
> *Abdullah*

The only element which is covered is the present. The reference to people coming to the party is not sufficient to cover this point and we do not know what they did at the party.

Sample answer E

Mark: 0

> *Dear my friend,*
> *I like come with they to there. I must to work and ther is no taim for it. I*
> *will to buy a computer for gifting and is verigood. My question is:*
> *1. where is parti?*
> *2. is who was there*
> *3. presents?*
> *Thank you*

The writer has not understood the task and does not provide answers to the questions in this reply.

Paper 2 Listening

Part 1

1 C   **2** A   **3** B   **4** C   **5** A

Part 2

6 G   **7** H   **8** C   **9** F   **10** D

Part 3

11 C   **12** B   **13** C   **14** A   **15** C

Part 4

For questions 16–20, ignore capitals / absence of capitals. Spelling must be correct.
16 September   **17** Jarvis   **18** 78 / seventy-eight (pounds)   **19** 223
20 bookshop / book shop

Part 5

For questions 21–25, ignore capitals / absence of capitals. Spelling must be correct,
except in questions 22 and 23, where recognisable spelling is acceptable.
21 9.30 / 21.30 / nine thirty / half past nine   **22** (the) entrance   **23** (the) lions
24 games   **25** 4.65 / four (pounds) (and) sixty-five (p/pence)

Transcript

This is the Cambridge Key English Test. Paper 2. Listening. Test number four. There are five parts to the test. Parts One, Two, Three, Four and Five. We will now stop for a moment before we start the test. Please ask any questions now because you mustn't speak during the test.

[pause]

PART 1   *Now, look at the instructions for Part One.*

[pause]

You will hear five short conversations. You will hear each conversation twice. There is one question for each conversation. For questions 1 to 5, put a tick under the right answer.

Here is an example:
How many people were at the meeting?

Woman:	Were there many people at the meeting?
Man:	About thirty.
Woman:	That's not many.
Man:	No, but more than last time.

[pause]

The answer is 30, so there is a tick in box C.
Now we are ready to start. Look at question one.

[pause]

Question 1   *One. How much is the car?*

Woman:	So which car are you buying?
Man:	The Monarch 2000. It's lovely but I have to get a thousand pounds more from the bank first because I don't have enough money.
Woman:	It's a lot of money ... three thousand pounds. I could live on that for a year.
Man:	Well, cars are expensive.

[pause]

Now listen again.

[repeat]

[pause]

Question 2   *Two. What's Elena going to take to the party?*

Man:	Hi, Elena. Are you taking some cans of cola to the party?
Elena:	Of course, and a pizza.
Man:	I'm going to take a big bottle of orange juice and some biscuits.
Elena:	Chocolate ones, I hope.

[pause]

Now listen again.

[repeat]

[pause]

Question 3   *Three. Where will Susan buy her eggs?*

Man: We need some more eggs, Susan.
Susan: I'll drive out to the farm and get them tomorrow.
Man: It'll be quicker to go to the market or to the little shop across the road.
Susan: I know, but I prefer to know that they haven't been on the shelves for
             a long time.

[pause]

Now listen again.

[repeat]

[pause]

Question 4   *Four. What time does the film begin?*

Woman: Would you like to see a film this afternoon?
Man: OK. What time?
Woman: It starts at quarter to two but we need tickets, so let's meet at the
             cinema at quarter past one.
Man: How long is the film?
Woman: One and a half hours.

[pause]

Now listen again.

[repeat]

[pause]

Question 5   *Five. How will the man travel to London?*

Woman: We drove to London last weekend.
Man: Really? I'm going to go there for the day tomorrow.
Woman: Oh yes? Are you going by coach?
Man: It's the best way. There's a fast train but it's too expensive for me.

[pause]

Now listen again.

[repeat]

[pause]

This is the end of Part One. Now look at Part Two.

[pause]

PART 2   *Listen to Sarah talking to a friend about a sports centre.*
             What is the problem with the different things at the sports centre?
             For questions 6 to 10, write a letter, A to H, next to each thing.
             You will hear the conversation twice.

[pause]

Friend: I like your new T-shirt, Sarah.
Sarah: Mm. The colours are nice, but the problem is it's too big. I got it from
             the shop at the sports centre. I went swimming there because it was

a hot day, but it was too noisy for me. There were a lot of people in the pool.

Friend: So was it difficult to find a space in the car park there?

Sarah: Yes! It's not big enough.

Friend: Did you go to the café?

Sarah: Yes, for a cold drink. But I didn't stay. The tables and floor weren't clean.

Friend: Ugh! But I hear they have a good football club there.

Sarah: That's right. My brother wanted to go but it starts too late in the evening for him. It's a pity because it's not an expensive club.

Friend: Can you learn tennis there?

Sarah: I called about lessons but they cost too much.

Friend: I'll teach you tennis – but not today – it's too hot. Let's go for a cold swim in the river.

[pause]

Now listen again.

[repeat]

[pause]

This is the end of Part Two. Now look at Part Three.

[pause]

PART 3   *Listen to Philip talking to a friend about his photography course.*
             For questions 11 to 15, tick A, B or C. You will hear the conversation twice.
             Look at questions 11 to 15 now. You have twenty seconds.

[pause]

Now listen to the conversation.

Friend: Hello, Philip. Are you doing a photography course?

Philip: Yes, there wasn't one at my college, Park College, so I go to City College in South Road.

Friend: Are your classes in the evening?

Philip: Yes, I finish at Park College at quarter past five and get home about six. The lessons start at quarter to seven. I have just enough time to eat.

Friend: How much are they?

Philip: My ten-week course is usually ninety-five pounds. But it costs me seventy-five pounds because I'm a student. There's also a five-week course for fifty-five pounds.

Friend: Is it a good course?

Philip: Yes, great. The cameras are rather old, but my photos are much better now, so I'm really pleased. I'll never be a famous photographer though.

Friend: I think taking photographs is difficult.

Philip: Well, we did animals first and they're certainly not easy. But then we took pictures of trees, and that wasn't difficult. We'll photograph children next.

Friend: And after the course?

Philip: There aren't many jobs for photographers. It'll be my hobby. I can use my father's camera but I'll have to buy a lot of film.

[pause]

Now listen again.

[repeat]

[pause]

This is the end of Part Three. Now look at Part Four.

[pause]

PART 4 *You will hear a man asking for information about the Westwood English School. Listen and complete questions 16 to 20. You will hear the conversation twice.*

[pause]

Woman: Westwood English School.

Man: Hello, I want to ask about evening classes, please.

Woman: Yes, they're on Thursdays. But this term will finish at the end of August. We'll start again on the twenty-second of September, but you can book your place now.

Man: It's for a Chinese friend. He wants an easy class.

Woman: Well, there's a two-hour class for beginners.

Man: Mmm. My friend would like something shorter.

Woman: Well, we have a fifty-minute speaking class. That would be good for him. The teacher is Miss Jarvis. That's J A R V I S. The students all like her.

Man: How much does that class cost?

Woman: It's seven pounds fifty per class or if you pay for all twelve classes now, it's only seventy-eight pounds – it's cheaper that way.

Man: Right.

Woman: Can your friend come to the school soon and book his place? The address is two hundred and twenty-three, Fitzroy Square.

Man: Is that in the centre of town?

Woman: Well, it's about twenty minutes' walk from the station. We're just by the bookshop.

Man: Right. Thank you.

Woman: Goodbye.

[pause]

Now listen again.

[repeat]

[pause]

This is the end of Part Four. Now look at Part Five.

[pause]

PART 5   *You will hear some information about Finchester Zoo.*
Listen and complete questions 21 to 25. You will hear the information twice.

[pause]

Woman: Thank you for calling Finchester Zoo. The zoo is open on six days and closed on Mondays. The opening hours are from ten a.m. until it gets dark. This is half past nine in the summer and four o'clock in the winter.

There is a guided tour of the zoo every hour. Visitors for the tour should wait at the entrance which is where the tour begins. Our guide will meet you there. The tour finishes at the café.

You should not feed the animals but you can watch when we give them something to eat. Every day at two o'clock the lions are given their food and the elephants get theirs at three o'clock.

There is a shop in the zoo where you can buy books and games. All the family will like playing these. There is also a café which sells snacks.

Tickets for adults cost six pounds eighty-five and children's tickets are four pounds sixty-five. A family ticket, for two adults and three children, is eighteen pounds seventy-five.

For more information ...

[pause]

Now listen again.

[repeat]

[pause]

This is the end of Part Five.

You now have eight minutes to write your answers on the answer sheet.

Note: Teacher, stop the recording here and time eight minutes. Remind the students when there is **one** minute remaining.

[pause]

This is the end of the test.

Sample answer sheet – Reading and Writing (Sheet 1)

UNIVERSITY *of* **CAMBRIDGE**
ESOL Examinations

S A M P L E

Candidate Name
If not already printed, write name
in CAPITALS and complete the
Candidate No. grid (in pencil).

Candidate Signature

Examination Title

Centre

Supervisor:

If the candidate is ABSENT or has WITHDRAWN shade here

Centre No.

Candidate No.

Examination
Details

0	0	0	0
1	1	1	1
2	2	2	2
3	3	3	3
4	4	4	4
5	5	5	5
6	6	6	6
7	7	7	7
8	8	8	8
9	9	9	9

KET Paper 1 Reading and Writing Candidate Answer Sheet

Instructions

Use a **PENCIL** (B or HB).
Rub out any answer you want to change with an eraser.

For **Parts 1, 2, 3, 4** and **5:**
Mark ONE letter for each question.
For example, if you think **C** is the right answer to the
question, mark your answer sheet like this:

| 0 | A B C |

Part 1

1	A B C D E F G H
2	A B C D E F G H
3	A B C D E F G H
4	A B C D E F G H
5	A B C D E F G H

Part 2

6	A B C
7	A B C
8	A B C
9	A B C
10	A B C

Part 3

11	A B C
12	A B C
13	A B C
14	A B C
15	A B C

16	A B C D E F G H
17	A B C D E F G H
18	A B C D E F G H
19	A B C D E F G H
20	A B C D E F G H

Part 4

21	A B C
22	A B C
23	A B C
24	A B C
25	A B C
26	A B C
27	A B C

Part 5

28	A B C
29	A B C
30	A B C
31	A B C
32	A B C
33	A B C
34	A B C
35	A B C

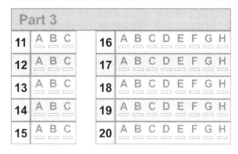
Turn over for
Parts 6 - 9 →

Sample answer sheet – Reading and Writing (Sheet 2)

For **Parts 6, 7 and 8:**

Write your answers in the spaces next to the numbers (36 to 55) like this:

| 0 | example ✏ |

Part 6		Do not write here
36		1 36 0
37		1 37 0
38		1 38 0
39		1 39 0
40		1 40 0

Part 7		Do not write here
41		1 41 0
42		1 42 0
43		1 43 0
44		1 44 0
45		1 45 0
46		1 46 0
47		1 47 0
48		1 48 0
49		1 49 0
50		1 50 0

Part 8		Do not write here
51		1 51 0
52		1 52 0
53		1 53 0
54		1 54 0
55		1 55 0

Part 9 (Question 56): Write your answer below.

Do not write below (Examiner use only)
0   1   2   3   4   5

Sample answer sheet – Listening

UNIVERSITY *of* CAMBRIDGE
ESOL Examinations

    SAMPLE

Candidate Name
If not already printed, write name
in CAPITALS and complete the
Candidate No. grid (in pencil)

Candidate Signature

Examination Title

Centre

Supervisor:

If the candidate is ABSENT or has WITHDRAWN shade here

Centre No.

Candidate No.

Examination Details

0	0	0	0
1	1	1	1
2	2	2	2
3	3	3	3
4	4	4	4
5	5	5	5
6	6	6	6
7	7	7	7
8	8	8	8
9	9	9	9

KET Paper 2 Listening Candidate Answer Sheet

Instructions

Use a PENCIL (B or HB).

Rub out any answer you want to change with an eraser.

For **Parts 1, 2** and **3**:
Mark ONE letter for each question.
For example, if you think **C** is the right answer to the
question, mark your answer sheet like this:

0 | A B C

Part 1	Part 2	Part 3
1 A B C	6 A B C D E F G H	11 A B C
2 A B C	7 A B C D E F G H	12 A B C
3 A B C	8 A B C D E F G H	13 A B C
4 A B C	9 A B C D E F G H	14 A B C
5 A B C	10 A B C D E F G H	15 A B C

For **Parts 4** and **5**:
Write your answers in the spaces next to the
numbers (16 to 25) like this:

0 | example

Part 4	Do not write here	Part 5	Do not write here
16	1 16 0	21	1 21 0
17	1 17 0	22	1 22 0
18	1 18 0	23	1 23 0
19	1 19 0	24	1 24 0
20	1 20 0	25	1 25 0

© UCLES 2006 Photocopiable

22518292R00082

Printed in Great Britain
by Amazon